Advanced Translation Practice German - English

von R. Eslava Cattliff

MANZ VERLAG MÜNCHEN

Herausgegeben von Ute Kretschmann

Manzbuch 533

6 5 4 3 2 1   1983 82 81 80
(Die jeweils letzte Zahl bezeichnet die Auflage bzw. das Erscheinungsjahr)

© 1980 by Manz Verlag, München. Alle Rechte vorbehalten.
Umschlagentwurf: Ingeburg Rothemund, München.
Gesamtherstellung: Verlag und Druckerei G. J. Manz AG, München/Dillingen.
Printed in Germany.

ISBN 3-7863-0533-1

Contents

Foreword 5

Abbrevations and Symbols 7

Section A: fairly difficult to difficult texts with English translation and annotations 8

Text 1: Ein englisches Modell für die Schule der Zukunft 8
Text 2: Der Arbeitsbeginn der sogenannten Open University . . 15
Text 3: aus "Geschichte von Isidor" 24

Section B: difficult texts — past examination texts of the "Fachliche Prüfung für das Lehramt an Realschulen" with translation and annotations 30

Text 1: Examination text 1976/I 30
Text 2: Examination text 1977/II 37
Text 3: Examination text 1978/I 44

Section C: difficult texts — past examination texts of the "Wissenschaftliche Prüfung für das Lehramt an den Gymnasien" with translation and annotations 52

Text 1: Examination text 1975/II 52
Text 2: Examination text 1976/I 64
Text 3: Examination text 1977/II 74

Section D: appendix — a selection of examination texts 84

Foreword

Purpose: this translation practice book is intended for advanced-level students of English whose native language is German. Although the texts and analysis might be used as a basis for course-work discussion it is primarily intended that this collection of texts and translation will be used for private study by students to supplement translation practice gained in class and to prepare for the German-English translation papers which are part of advanced-level examinations, such as the Zwischenprüfung, die fachliche Prüfung für das Lehramt an Realschulen, die wissenschaftliche Prüfung für das Lehramt an den Gymnasien. It is not a "crash course" in German-English translation. Translation skills are assimilated over a long period of steady practice. This book contains a selection of German texts and possible English translations, carefully annotated, to help contribute towards the acquisition of such translation skills.

Choice of texts: the texts, apart from a few exceptions taken from German literature, deal with some aspect of British or American life, as is typical of the majority of texts presented in the Bavarian state examinations for future Realschul- and Gymnasiallehrer. I have tried to place the texts in order of difficulty. They are divided into four sections: A — fairly difficult to difficult texts containing a variety of structural problems for translation, which could be used as preparation for the Zwischenprüfung; B — past examination texts set by the Bavarian Ministry of Education for the Fachliche Prüfung für das Lehramt an Realschulen. Note that the time allowed for these texts was 2 hours. C — past examination papers set by the Bavarian Ministry of Education for the Wissenschaftliche Prüfung für das Lehramt an den Gymnasien. The time allowed for these texts was 3 hours. Section D, the appendix, contains extra text examples, untranslated, of the two above-mentioned examinations.

Unit structure: each "unit" begins with a German text followed, where appropriate, by a word of warning about particular translation difficulties presented by the text. Next, where considered useful, follow cultural background notes on institutions mentioned in the text. A "model" translation is then provided in sections, each of which is accompanied by detailed annotations. The "model" translation is only one of possibly several good or acceptable versions. As many alternatives as possible are offered in the annotations together with discussion of wrong or unsuitable translations. These annotations, comprehensive but not, of course, exhaustive, are based on the experience of many translation courses held with German university students of English.

References: students are frequently referred to Quirk, Greenbaum: A University Grammar of English (hereafter UGE), in particular to chapter 8 on Adjuncts, Disjuncts, Conjuncts and to chapter 14 on Focus, Theme and Emphasis, both of which could be regarded as recommended reading before embarking on work with this book. In the annotations any notes on grammar are only sketchy and students should thus have recourse to a reliable grammar reference book for a detailed study.

Acknowledgements: I am grateful to my students at Augsburg University for providing much of the material included in the annotations during the course of class discussion and in their written tests. I should also like to thank my colleagues and friends at Augsburg for helping me with many questions of interpretation of the German text and with the translations. My thanks go especially to Cecilia Salmonson for proofreading the script and for her invaluable criticisms and suggestions.

Roslyn Eslava Cattliff
Augsburg, October 1979

Abbreviations and Symbols

Note: In the annotations the line-numbers refer to numbering of the German source text.

+	=	item which follows is: correct
(+)	=	also correct, but inferior to +
×	=	unsuitable in this context
⊗	=	term/idiom/structure incorrect
,	=	comma obligatory or desirable stylistically
(,)	=	comma optional
/	=	marks beginning of an alternative translation
[ ]	=	optional material in English translation, i.e. may be omitted
( )	=	(in annotations) explanation of item
ST	=	source text
ET	=	English translation
BE	=	British English
AmE	=	American English
fig.	=	figurative(ly)
lit.	=	literal(ly)
s.th.	=	something
esp.	=	especially
approx.	=	approximate(ly)
c.f.	=	compare
UGE	=	Quirk R., Greenbaum S.: A University Grammar of English (Longman, 1973)

Section A

Text 1

Ein englisches Modell für die Schule der Zukunft

Die Comprehensive School[1] wurde nach dem Krieg von den Sozialisten in England eingeführt und hat noch heute mit dem leidenschaftlichen Widerstand des traditionellen Schulwesens[2] und seiner um dessen Existenz bangenden Vertreter zu
5 kämpfen. Immer wieder kommt es zu turbulenten Demonstrationen, wenn irgendwo in Großbritannien eine der alten, traditionsreichen Grammar Schools[3] durch eine Comprehensive School ersetzt werden soll, die etwa der deutschen Gesamtschule entspricht. Wenn die Comprehensive School sich auf
10 die Dauer durchsetzt, wird sie alle anderen Schultypen überflüssig machen.
Der Aufbau einer solchen Schule ist zugleich kompliziert und genial einfach. Eine Reihe von traditionellen englischen Schulcharakteristiken, wie etwa das pädagogisch bewährte
15 Housemaster[4]- und Tutoren[5]-System, wird beibehalten.
Jedem Kind, das mit zehn oder elf Jahren die fünfklassige Grundschule[6] verläßt, soll durch diese Schule die Möglichkeit geboten werden, eine seinen Anlagen und seinem Interesse entsprechende Ausbildung zu erhalten, ohne sich schon
20 im Kindesalter entscheiden zu müssen, ob es den geistesoder naturwissenschaftlichen Zweig oder überhaupt eine höhere Schule besuchen will.

Heidewig Fankhänel, Die Zeit (adapted)

Cultural Notes

1. **Comprehensive School:** large school providing all types of state-run secondary education (i.e. age-group 11–16/18) in Britain. The Comprehensive School system has been promoted by Labour governments.

2. **des traditionellen Schulwesens:** traditionally secondary education in state schools in Britain was divided into three branches: grammar schools[3] (for pupils of high academic ability, selected formerly by the 11 + examination taken at the age of about 10), secondary modern, and technical schools (the two latter placing greater emphasis on subjects which are more practical but less academic).

3. **Grammar Schools:** see note 2 above.

4. **Housemaster-System:** British schools, whether state- or privately run, traditionally have subdivisions into "houses" (possibly four to six depending on the size of the establishment). On entering the school each pupil becomes a member of a house and remains such for the duration of his school studies. Each house is presided over by a housemaster, who is responsible for giving his house-members moral or academic advice, organising sports and other activities with other houses. An important motive underlying the house system is to provide pupils with affiliations beyond those of the form to which they belong by virtue of their age and/or ability.

5. **Tutoren-System:** system by which pupils are taught at frequent intervals individually or in very small groups by the tutor assigned to them.

6. **die fünfklassige Grundschule:** children are legally obliged to attend school from the age of 5 to 16. The first five years are spent at primary school, which is subdivided into the infant school (for 5 to 7-year-olds) and the junior school (for 7 to 10/11-year-olds).

"Model" translation(s) and annotations (in sections)

An English model for the school of the future.

> The Comprehensive School was introduced in England by the Socialists after the war and [even] today [it] still has to contend with impassioned resistance from the traditional school system and its supporters, who are anxious about the latter type of school's future.

II. 1—2 nach dem Krieg von den Sozialisten in England: take care with the relative position of these 3 prepositional phrases. In particular avoid placing "in England" after the agent "Socialists". Otherwise the adverbial of place may be interpreted as a postmodifier of "socialists".

Stylistically it is preferable to place the time adjunct at the end of this clause to provide a stronger link to the subsequent clause introduced with the time adjunct "even today".

l. 2 noch heute: "still" should be placed medially, i.e. within the verb phrase, rather than in the very unusual position premodifying "today". The latter position is, however, suitable for "even": + *even today.*

ll. 2—5 hat mit ... zu kämpfen: + *is still up against;* + *still has to struggle with.* (Note that "still" must follow the verb "to be" used unemphatically.)

l. 3 leidenschaftlichen: + *fierce;* + *passionate;* + *vehement;* + *keen;* (+) *enthusiastic* (collocation with "resistance" not usual. cf. enthusiastic response, welcome, acceptance, support).

ll. 2—3 mit dem ... Widerstand des ... Schulwesens: note use of definite article with abstract noun "resistance" **only** if postmodified by "of"-prepositional phrase: + *with the fierce resistance of the traditional school system.*

l. 4 Vertreter: + *advocates;* + *champions;* × *representatives* (not the meaning in this context).

l. 4 seiner um ... bangenden Vertreter: ⊗ *and its about the latter type of school's future anxious supporters.* It should be (horribly) clear that this ET attempt is **absolutely wrong.** The long pre-modifying attributive phrase in ST cannot be rendered in ET by a similar construction. What is required is a post-modifying relative clause: + *and its supporters, who are anxious about ....* . Note that comma and wh-relative pronoun are obligatory (non-defining relative clause).

— **l. 4 dessen:** (+) *its* (stylistically poor as reference of possessive determiner not absolutely clear. Besides this would mean repetition of the word "its". This passage reads more clearly if ET uses: + *the latter type of school's.*

— **l. 4 Existenz:** + *continued existence;* × *existence.* (It is the future existence and not the present existence of the traditional school system that is referred to here.)

l. 4 um ... bangen: + *worried about;* + *concerned about;* × *anxious/ worried/concerned for* (cf. I'm worried for him — he may fail the exam. (= worried on his behalf.)

> Again and again there are stormy demonstrations whenever somewhere in Great Britain one of the old Grammar Schools, abundant in tradition, is to be replaced by a Comprehensive School, which is

more or less equivalent to the German "Gesamtschule". If the Comprehensive School proves itself in the long term, it will render all other types of school superfluous.

I. 5 turbulent: + *turbulent;* + *noisy;* + *boisterous;* × *violent* (would mean that violence is used, which is not necessarily implied by the German text and which is not borne out by actual events); × *tempestuous* (rather poetic; usually used of weather, temperament).

II. 5—6 Immer wieder kommt es zu turbulenten Demonstrationen: + *Again and again stormy demonstrations take place;* + *Stormy demonstrations frequently occur when(ever)...;* + *Stormy demonstrations occur repeatedly.../repeatedly occur....*

I. 6 wenn: + *when;* (+) *if.*

II. 6—7 traditionsreich: × *traditional.* A phrase post-modifying "Grammar Schools", placed between commas, is required here: + *with their many traditions;* + *with their wealth of tradition;* + *full of tradition(s);* + *rich in tradition(s).*

II. 6—7 wenn ... Schools: word order: owing to the placing of the above insertion after "Grammar Schools" it is preferable to introduce the place adjunct before the subject of the clause: +*...whenever somewhere in Great Britain one of the old Grammar Schools, abundant in tradition, is....* Otherwise the ET would read: (+) *whenever one of the old Grammar Schools, abundant in tradition, somewhere in Great Britain is....* Take care too that the relative clause ET follows directly on "Comprehensive School" so that there is no ambiguity of reference.

I. 8 soll: × *should* (would express obligation). Here "soll" expresses an intention or plan, probably formed by public authorities.

II. 8—9..., die ... entspricht: A non-defining relative clause. The comma is therefore obligatory in ET.

I. 8 etwa: + *approximately;* + *about;* + *roughly* (more informal).

I. 9 entspricht: + *is comparable with;* + *corresponds to;* × *complies with* (demands; regulations); × *meets* (demands; requirements).

II. 9—10 sich ... durchsetzt: + *proves its worth;* + *is successful;* + *wins/gains favour;* + *prevails.*

II. 9—10 auf die Dauer: + *in the long run;* × *permanently* (not here).

II. 10—11 überflüssig machen: + *make superfluous;* + *supersede;* (+) *render/make redundant* (usually in connection with dismissals from work); × *render/make unnecessary.*

l. 10 wird: owing to the presence of the if-clause it is most likely that a "will"-future will be employed here. Not impossible, however, is the "going to" form, as a feeling of certainty about future events is expressed here. Other forms of the future are, however, precluded.

> The structure of such a school is at once complex and ingeniously simple. A number of traditional characteristics of English schools, as for instance the pedagogically approved housemaster and tutor system, has been retained.

— **l. 12 ist zugleich ... und ...:** + *is both ... and ...;* + *is at the same time ... and ....*

— **l. 13 genial einfach:** the German "genial" (= gifted; ingenious) has nothing to do with the English "genial" (= kindly; sympathetic; sociable).

— **l. 13 Eine Reihe:** + *a string;* + *a succession;* (+) *a series* (suggests progression); × *a set* (suggests all items of absolute group are included); × *a range* (suggests selection of items to present a cross-section).

ll. 13—14 von traditionellen englischen Schulcharakteristiken: (+) *of traditional English school characteristics* (rather unidiomatic; stylistically phrase unbalanced).

l. 14 wie etwa: + *such as;* × *like* (strictly speaking would mean "similar to" thus ungrammatical here, even though frequently heard in "carelessly expressed" spoken English).

— **l. 14 bewährte:** (+) *proven;* (+) *proved* (Can a system really be proven? It can prove itself or it can prove worthwhile, etc.); (+) *sound* (suggests greater degree of acceptance than in ST); × *tried;* × *tested.*

— **ll. 14—15 das pädagogisch bewährte Housemaster- und Tutorensystem:** + *...the housemaster and tutor system, which has proved itself from a pedagogical point of view,/pedagogically, ...;* + *...the housemaster and tutor system, which has proved to be pedagogically sound.*

l. 15 wird beibehalten: (a) tense: preferably present perfect but simple present also possible. (b) + *maintained;* + *preserved;* + *continued;* (+) *kept up* (more informal). (c) + *have been retained* (plural verb also appropriate as reference is made to a plurality).

> The Comprehensive School is supposed to offer every ten or eleven-year-old [child] who has completed the five forms of primary school the opportunity of receiving a type of education compatible

with his talents and interests without the pupil's having to decide at a very early age whether he wishes to go in for arts or sciences or whether he wishes to attend a grammar school at all.

I. 17 diese Schule: + *this school;* + *this type of school* (In the interests of lucidity, I prefer to use the full term "Comprehensive School" here, as it is some lines since it was mentioned).

II. 16—18 Jedem Kind ... geboten werden: + *Upon completion of the five forms of primary school every ten or eleven-year-old is supposed to be offered the opportunity at the Comprehensive School of...;* + *Every ten or eleven-year-old leaving the five-form primary school/ leaving the primary school after completing the five forms is supposed to....*

II. 17—18 soll die Möglichkeit geboten werden ... zu erhalten: + *is supposed to be given/provided with the opportunity/chance of receiving/to receive....*

I. 16 mit zehn oder elf Jahren: + *at the age of ten or eleven;* ⊗ *in the age of ten or eleven* (cf. *in the Elizabethan Age; in the Middle Ages*).

II. 16—17 die fünfklassige Grundschule: (+) *grades* (AmE); see also cultural notes above.

II. 18—19 eine seinen Anlagen und seinem Interesse entsprechende Ausbildung: avoid the common mistake of attempting to render this long and weighty pre-modifying attributive phrase in ST by a similar construction in ET. While a single, or series of adjectives may, of course, premodify the noun, it is impossible to introduce a prepositional phrase in this position. Recourse must be made to post-modifying prepositional or participial phrases, relative clauses, reduced relative clauses, insertions. ET may thus read: (a) **entsprechende:** + *a suitable type of education for his talents and interests* ("interests" usually plural in English idiom); + *a type of education suited to/suitable to/that suits/geared to/in accordance with his talents and interests:* × *matching* (2 items must show closer identity); × *conforming to* (standards, customs, etiquette, conventions, patterns, etc.); × *complying with* (demands, requests, wishes); × *meeting* (demands); × *corresponding to* (expectations). (b) **Anlagen:** + *abilities;* (+) *gifts* (not very suitable in this context).

II. 19—20 ohne sich ... entscheiden zu müssen: if the subject of your main clause is "The Comprehensive School"/"This school", you must give the participle "having to" a subject of its own (+ *without his*

having to; × *without having to*) in order to avoid the common error of misreference of participle (e.g. ⊗ Walking along the road a brick fell on my head!). Remember that if a participle has no subject of its own its subject is automatically that of the main clause. There is, of course, no problem if the subject of your main clause is: "Every child"/"Every ten or eleven-year-old". Thus: + *Every ten or eleven-year-old ... is supposed to be offered the opportunity of receiving an education ... without having to decide/without his having to decide....*
II. 19—20 schon im Kindesalter: + *at an impossibly early age.*
II. 20—21 den geistes- oder naturwissenschaftlichen Zweig: + *the Arts or the Sciences.* (In Britain this did not involve a choice between different schools.)
II. 21—22 eine höhere Schule: × *high school* (AmE, therefore not really suitable for this text on Britain); × *secondary school* (this term includes all forms of school education from age 11—16/18. Thus, with compulsory education up to the age of 16, the child has no option but to attend secondary school). × *higher school* (unidiomatic. cf. higher education = education after age of 16/18 e.g. college, university). × *gymnasium* (= hall for gymnastics).
l. 22 besuchen: × *visit* (= not as a pupil).
l. 22 will: + *wants to* (more informal); × *will* (pure futurity).

Text 2

Der Arbeitsbeginn der sogenannten Open University[1] in England, einer akademischen Fortbildungsinstitution, die mit Fernsehkursen, Lehrbriefen und einem dichten Netz von Tutoren Angehörigen der Mittel- und der Arbeitsklasse bessere
5 Bildungschancen geben will, ist eine neue Stufe in einem Wandlungsprozeß des intellektuellen Lebens in Großbritannien, der hierzulande zur Kenntnis genommen wurde, dessen Auswirkungen aber sicher weitreichend sein werden.
Von 1945 bis 1955 lebten die englischen Intellektuellen in
10 einer eigenartigen Isolierung; der Übergang von vorübergehender Beschäftigung in der Kriegsmaschinerie zum normalisierten Nachkriegsleben vollzog sich fast reibungslos. Das erste Jahrzehnt nach dem Krieg war eine Zeit der Introversion gewesen, des Anschlußfindens an eine verloren-
15 geglaubte, aber unzerstörte Tradition.
Um die Mitte der fünfziger Jahre begann sich ein Ende der insularen Beschränkung abzuzeichnen. Die "affluent society" hatte ihre prägnanteste Phase erreicht. Konsumgüterverbrauch und Motorisierung hatten rapide zugenommen, Ferienreisen
20 waren für fast jedermann erschwinglich, das Fernsehen war in jedes zweite Wohnzimmer eingedrungen. Die Auswirkungen dieser Entwicklung waren drastisch. Reklame und Werbung beherrschten weite Teile des öffentlichen Lebens. Jugend und Sex wurden zu Kultobjekten erhoben. Gleichzeitig erlebten
25 die Universitäten eine Expansion, wie man sie seit der Jahrhundertwende nicht mehr gekannt hatte. Zu den beiden Typen Oxbridge[2] und Redbrick[3] trat nun die "new university"[4], und Neugründungen wie Sussex oder Norwich laufen, was die Attraktivität bei englischen Abiturienten angeht, beinahe
30 Oxford und Cambridge den Rang ab. Interdisziplinäre Studien, Verhaltensforschung und Soziologie gehörten bald zu den herausragenden Leistungen der neuen Universitäten. Die Rollkragenpullover und Lederjacken in Hörsälen und Theatern haben die Vorherrschaft des traditionellen Public-
35 School[5]-Ethos über das intellektuelle Leben gebrochen. Die jungen Historiker, Literaturkritiker und Soziologen, die jungen Theater-, Film- und Fernsehleute vertreten zum ersten-

mal eine Bevölkerungsschicht, der bislang die Teilnahme am kulturellen Leben des Landes weitgehend verweigert war und der nun mit der Open University eine ganz neue Chance gegeben ist. Man darf gespannt sein, ob und wie sie sie nutzen wird.

Süddeutsche Zeitung (21. 1. 1971)

Cultural Notes

1. The **Open University** offers degree courses by means of television, radio, and correspondence courses. Students usually spend about one week per year at one of the university's summer schools. It is often referred to as "university of the air". It is comparable to Germany's "Telekolleg".

2. **Oxbridge.** By this compound is meant the universities of Oxford and Cambridge. Dating from 1249 and 1284 respectively they are the oldest British universities and until the nineteenth century they were the only two universities in **England**. (In Scotland four universities were founded in the fourteenth and fifteenth centuries.) The universities of Oxford and Cambridge, unlike other British universities, are organised on the college system.

3. **Redbrick.** The Redbrick universities include all the universities founded in the nineteenth and early twentieth centuries. They are situated in London and the industrial cities that developed in that period. They take their name from the building material predominantly used at that time.

4. **"New University".** These are the universities founded since the second World War, and especially since the early 1960s. Among them are, for example, the universities of Sussex (at Brighton), East Anglie (at Norwich), Essex (at Colchester). Most of them are campus-style universities.

5. Public Schools are the most famous of Britain's private schools. Particularly well-known are Eton College (the oldest, founded in 1440), Harrow, Winchester, and Rugby. Their name is derived from the circumstances in which the first public school developed —

namely to provide free education to talented boys whose parents could not afford to employ a private tutor in the home. They are mostly boarding schools. Traditionally great emphasis is placed on sports, through which, it was (is) widely believed, the development of personality and character (fair play, team spirit, endurance, perseverance, qualities of leadership, etc.) could be fostered. Public schools have produced many of Britain's leading politicians and other distinguished men. Nowadays, they are criticised by many people who see in them a continuation of privilege and a bastion of Britain's upper and wealthy classes.

"Model" translation(s) and annotations (in sections)

The opening of the so-called Open University in Britain, an academic institution for further education, which by means of television and correspondence courses(,) and a close network of tutors aims to provide members of the middle and working classes with better educational opportunities, marks a new stage in a process of change of intellectual life in Great Britain(,) which has been noted here and which will certainly have far-reaching consequences.

I. 1 Arbeitsbeginn: × *beginning of work* (= when each day's work/when a project begins); × *putting into operation* (= of a machine); × *putting into force* (= a regulation, a law).
II. 1—2 England: probably "England" is used here imprecisely, and the reference is to the whole of Britain (including Scotland, Wales and Northern Ireland).
I. 2 Fortbildungsinstitution: + *institution for/of higher education;* + *higher/further education institution.* × *establishment* (suggests reference to a specific school/building e.g. "St. Bede's is an educational establishment for the daughters of Anglican clergymen"). Note: no definite article with general reference of 'education'.
I. 2 mit: + *with the aid of/with;* × *with the help of* (suited to more "practical" context e.g. with the help of a jack we managed to get the car out of the soft sand).
II. 3—4 Tutoren: + *teachers/instructors* (rather typical of AmE; in BE "instructor" usually used for sports or practical activities: e.g. ski instructor, driving instructor).

17

l. 4 will: + *intends to;* + *sets out to;* × *wants to* (too emotional/personal).

l. 5 Bildungschancen: with general reference to education and careers the word + *opportunities* is preferable to × *chances* ('He's got many chances' = he's got many separate opportunities to do s.th.); × *prospects* e.g. career prospects (= chances of promotion), business prospects (= chances of doing business/winning contracts).

l. 5 ist: + *is;* + *means;* × *represents.*

l. 5 Stufe: + *step.*

l. 6 Wandlungsprozeß: "Wandlung" suggests an extensive but gradual change, probably developing from within (cf. Veränderung, which may denote a small or extensive change, but probably imposed from without e.g. by law). Thus: + *process of transition of/in...* (= gradual process; neutral intensity); + *process of change of/in...* (= neutral both as far as speed and intensity of the change are concerned); + *process of transformation of...* (= extensive change; neutral as far as speed of change is concerned).

l. 5 des intellektuellen Lebens: note: no definite article (otherwise reference too specific; cf. "social life in England" (general reference — as opposed to e.g. economic life) **but** "the social life is very good at our university" (more specific reference = social activities, dances, parties, etc.). However, if a prepositional postmodifier phrase beginning with the preposition "of" is used, it is acceptable to use definite article: + *the intellectual life of Great Britain.* Avoid juxtaposition of 3 'of' phrases.

l. 5 punctuation: comma after "Great Britain" optional as the following relative clause can be interpreted as being essential (without comma) or non-essential (with comma).

ll. 5—6 hierzulande: + *in this/our country.*

l. 6 genommen wurde: note Present Perfect tense necessary here (acknowledgement of the change not related to a specific past time — simply at some point before the present moment of writing).

ll. 6—7 dessen Auswirkungen aber sicher weitreichend sein werden: (+) *whose consequences will certainly be far-reaching* (less idiomatic than model); (+) *the consequences of which will certainly be far-reaching.*

l. 6 aber: better left untranslated as no logical contrast is actually apparent; link the two clauses with "and".

l. 6 sicher: (+) *surely* (not so suitable here as "surely" is used to appeal for confirmation of one's opinion rather than to intensify the certainty of one's view); × *definitely* (sounds too certain/authoritarian).

From 1945 to 1955, British intellectuals lived in a curious sort of isolation; the transition from temporarily being part of the machinery of war to normalised post-war life took place quite smoothly. The first decade after the war had been a period of introversion, of finding the way back to a tradition which was believed lost but which had remained intact.

l. 8 die englischen Intellektuellen: (cf. l. 5 above). Omit definite article as "British/English (cf. l. 1 above) intellectuals" are referred to here in general. "The British intellectuals" would suggest that there was a very definite, specific group of intellectuals.

ll. 9—10 in einer ... Isolierung: "isolation" uncountable: × *a curious isolation*. To render countable add: + *a ... sort of .../a ... kind of .../ a ... type of ...* .

l. 10 eigenartig: + *strange*; + *peculiar*; + *unusual*; (+) *odd*; × *weird* (too exaggerated. Also note that 'weird' tends to be over-used in modern informal spoken English and should therefore be avoided in formal written style); × *queer* (too exaggerated/too informal; used in modern colloquial idiom to mean "homosexual").

ll. 10—11 von vorübergehender Beschäftigung in der Kriegsmaschinerie: + *from temporary employment in the machinery of war/in the war machinery*; (+) *in the industry of war*.

l. 12 vollzog sich: + *occurred*; + *was carried out*; (+) *came about*; (+) *came off* (rather informal).

l. 12 fast reibungslos: + *almost without any problem(s)*; (+) *almost without any hitch* (too informal?); × *almost smoothly*; × *nearly without any problem* ("nearly" only used in connection with a specific point of reference e.g. "we're nearly there/at home/in Doncaster/finished/16 years old". "Almost" can be used in the latter cases and also with vaguer reference e.g. "she was almost happy"/"I almost enjoyed the party" [in which cases "nearly" cannot be used]. If in doubt, use "almost"!).

l. 14 des Anschlußfindens an ... : (a) preposition "of" must be repeated, otherwise the clause would read as a participial clause of time or reason. (b) + *of finding one's way back to*; + *of returning to*.

ll. 14—15 eine verlorengeglaubte, aber unzerstörte Tradition: lengthy pre-modifying attributive in German must here be rendered by a relative clause in English (essential, thus no comma!). See also text A1, l. 4 and ll. 18—19, and text A3, ll. 9—10 and ll. 16—18.

l. 15 unzerstörte: + *which had not been destroyed;* × *undestroyed.*

> Around the mid-fifties an end of insular confinement gradually became evident. The 'affluent society' had reached its peak. The purchase of consumer goods and motorisation had rapidly increased; holiday trips were within almost everyone's means(,) and television had forced its way into every other living-room. The effects of this development were drastic. Advertising and publicity dominated wide areas of public life. Youth and sex were exalted to objects of cult.

l. 16 um die Mitte der fünfziger Jahre: + *around the middle of the fifties;* ⊗ *around the middle of the fifty years.*
ll. 16—17 der insularen Beschränkung: + *of the insular confinement.*
ll. 16—17 begann sich ... abzuzeichnen: + *began to be felt;* + *began to make itself felt.* ((+) *started* ... [stylistically inferior].)
l. 18 Konsumgüterverbrauch: + *the purchasing of consumer goods.*
l. 19 zugenommen: + *spread.*
ll. 19—20 Ferienreisen waren für fast jedermann erschwinglich: (a) + *holiday travel was* ... (Note: uncountable!); × *holiday journeys.* (b) + *almost everyone could afford holiday trips.*
ll. 20—21 das Fernsehen war in jedes zweite Wohnzimmer eingedrungen: (a) (+) *the television* (More likely without article as reference here is to general, abstract concept.). (b) + *had invaded every...;* + *had intruded into every ....* (c) + *every second living room.* (d) + *sitting room;* × *parlour* (too old-fashioned); × *lounge* (expression not neutral = elevated expression for sitting room in private house; otherwise used for public buildings e.g. hotel, pub, airport, etc.).
l. 21 Auswirkungen: + *consequences;* (+) *repercussions* (not neutral — suggests negative consequences).
l. 22 drastisch: × *considerable.*
l. 22 Reklame und Werbung: × *advertisements* (reference is to series of individual advertisements, rather than to a general concept); × *adverts* (= abbreviation of 'advertisements').
l. 23 weite Teile: + *wide areas/spheres/sectors/sections;* + *vast areas/ sectors/sections.*
l. 23 des öffentlichen Lebens: Note: no definite article (cf. l. 5).

l. 24 **wurden ... erhoben:** + *were elevated to;* + *were raised to;* + *were set up as;* + *were adopted as.*
l. 24 **Kultobjekten:** + *cult objects;* × *cultural objects.*

> At the same time the universities underwent an expansion(,) the like of which had not been experienced since the turn of the century. The Oxbridge and Redbrick types were now joined by the 'new university'(,) and new foundations such as Sussex and Norwich are almost outstripping Oxford and Cambridge in their popularity among sixth-formers. Interdisciplinary studies, behaviour research, and sociology soon ranked among the outstanding achievements of the new universities.

l. 24 **Gleichzeitig:** × *simultaneously* (reference too limited).
l. 24 **erlebten:** (a) + *were undergoing* (either aspect appropriate, whereby use of progressive aspect suggests a more gradual, longer process of change than if simple aspect is employed. (b) + *saw;* + *witnessed;* + *experienced* (if not used in following clause).
l. 25 **Expansion:** × *extension* (too concrete: "the university is being extended" = more buildings are being added).
l. 25 **punctuation:** comma optional, as succeeding relative clause can be interpreted as essential (without comma) or non-essential (with comma).
ll. 25—26 **wie man sie ... nicht mehr gekannt hatte:** + *such as had not been known/experienced/seen;* + *as had not been known;* × *as it had not been known* (= dependent clause of reason).
ll. 26—27 **Zu den beiden Typen Oxbridge und Redbrick trat nun die 'new university':** (a) + *The "new university" joined the Oxbridge and Redbrick types* (first "model" translation superior, however, as the "new university", which is the main piece of information in the clause, takes up the usual (= final) position for the information focus. (See UGE chap. 14.) Besides, the link to the succeeding clause, which deals with new universities, is closer and thus neater. (b) Tense: either Simple Past or Present Perfect.
ll. 28—30 **laufen ... den Rang ab:** (a) Aspect: both progressive and simple aspects acceptable, (b) + *outdo;* + *surpass;* + *exceed;* (+) *get the better of* (rather informal).
l. 29 **beinahe:** + *nearly* (more informal).
l. 29 **bei englischen Abiturienten:** (a) + *popularity* + *among/amongst;* + *attractivenes* + *among/amongst/for.* (b) + *A-level candidates;* ×

school-leavers (could be of any age from 16 on; may not have taken or may not intend to take G.C.E. A-level examinations).
II. 28—29 was die Attraktivität ... angeht: (a) + *in popularity.* (b) + *in attractiveness;* × *in attraction.* (c) + *as far as (their) popularity ... is concerned.*
I. 31 Verhaltensforschung: + *behavioural research;* + *behaviour science.*
I. 31 gehörten bald zu: + *were soon among;* + *soon figured among;* × *soon belonged to.*
I. 32 herausragenden: + *distinguished;* (+) *prominent.*
I. 32 Leistungen: × *accomplishments* (usually with personal reference); × *efficiency* (= executing much work in little time/without wastage of energy resources e.g. of a machine, a person, an organisation).

> Polo-necked sweaters and leather jackets in lecture-halls and theatres have broken the supremacy of the public-school ethos over intellectual life. Young historians, literary critics(,) and sociologists, young people in the theatre, film and television world represent for the first time a section of the population which, to a large extent, has hitherto been denied participation in the country's cultural life and which is now given a completely new chance through the Open University. One cannot help wondering whether and how they are going to take advantage of it.

I. 33 Rollkragenpullover: (a) + *polo-neck/turtle-neck(ed) sweaters/pullovers/jumpers;* (b) no definite article (general sense).
I. 33 Hörsälen: + *auditoriums.*
I. 34 die Vorherrschaft: + *predominance;* + *predominancy.*
I. 35 gebrochen: + *broken down;* + *destroyed.*
II. 35—37 Die jungen Historiker, ..., die jungen Theater-, Film- und Fernsehleute: (a) no definite articles in English ("young" not functioning as a defining/contrastive adjective here). (b) + *young people working in/for the theatre, film and television world(s)/branches;* + *young people in the theatre, in films and television.*
I. 38 bislang: + *so far.*
II. 38—39 der ... die Teilnahme ... verweigert war: + *which has not been permitted to participate in ... .*
I. 39 am kulturellen Leben des Landes: (+) *in the cultural life of the country* (inferior because ambiguous meaning of "country" when

placed in this end-focus position: = (a) + *nation;* (b) × *countryside;* × *rural areas).*
I. 40 mit der Open University: + *in the form of the Open University;* + *with the Open University* (in latter case beware of position of prepositional phrase! Do not place after "chance" as will read as postmodifier of this noun (× *given a completely new chance with the Open University).* Use following word order and punctuation: + *and which, with the new Open University, has been given a completely new chance.*
I. 41 gegeben ist: + *has been given.*
I. 41 Man darf gespannt sein: + *One wonders;* + *Let's see.*
II. 41—42 ob und wie sie sie nutzen wird: (a) + *they will take advantage of it;* (b) + *if and in what way...;* (c) + *will make use of it;* + *will use it.*

Text 3

"Isidor!" fragte sie, "wo bist du nur so lang gewesen?"
Der Mann, einen Augenblick lang wie betäubt, setzte seine
Tasse nieder; er war es einfach nicht mehr gewohnt, verheiratet zu sein, und stellte sich vor einen Rosenstock,
5   die Hände in den Hosentaschen. "Warum hast du nie auch nur
eine Karte geschrieben?" fragte sie. Darauf nahm er den verdutzten Kindern wortlos den Tropenhelm weg, setzte ihn mit
dem knappen Schwung der Routine auf seinen eigenen Kopf,
was den Kindern einen für die Dauer ihres Lebens unauslösch-
10 lichen Eindruck hinterlassen haben soll, Papi mit Tropenhelm und Revolvertasche, alles nicht bloß echt, sondern
sichtlich vom Gebrauche etwas abgenutzt, und als die Gattin
sagte: "Weißt du, Isidor, das hättest du wirklich nicht tun
dürfen!" war es für Isidor genug der trauten Heimkehr, er
15 zog (wieder mit dem knappen Schwung der Routine, denke ich)
den Revolver aus dem Gurt, gab drei Schüsse mitten in die
weiche, bisher noch unberührte und mit Zuckerschaum ver-
zierte Torte, was, wie man sich wohl vorstellen kann, eine
erhebliche Schweinerei verursachte.

Max Frisch: aus "Geschichte von Isidor"

Particular difficulties in this text are presented by lengthy pre-nominal attributive phrases in German (ll. 9—10; ll. 16—18), which need to be rendered into English by means of post-modifying prepositional and participial phrases, relative clauses in addition to adjective pre-modification.

"Model" translation(s) and annotations (in sections)

> "Isidor!" she cried. "Where on earth have you been all this time?"
> The man, as if momentarily stunned, put his cup down; he simply was not accustomed to being a married man any more. He took up a position in front of a rose-bush, his hands in his trouser(-) pockets.

l. 1 fragte: to avoid using asked or inquired between the exclamation "Isidor!" and the subsequent question, in which case the choice of verb would be inappropriate as it would refer back to the exclamation rather than to what follows, either: (a) substitute a verb appropriate to exclamation, e.g. + *blurted out* (very abrupt), + *cried*. ("Screamed" is rather too dramatic for this stage of events!) Use a full-stop after the verb. Or (b) retain + *asked* or + *inquired* but place after the question so that the sentence reads: + *"Isidor! Where on earth have you been all this time?" she asked/inquired.*

I. 1 wo ... nur: to render the intensification of "where", expressed in ST by "nur", use an idiomatic phrase such as: + *where in the world...;* + *where on earth...;* + *wherever.*

I. 1 so lang: in a Wh-question it is usual to use the phrase **all this time,** as in "What have you been doing all this time?" Statements tend to make use of either "so long" or "all this time", as in "you've been away so long/all this time!"

I. 1 bist du ... gewesen: present perfect tense is obligatory here, the time reference being to a period of time extending from the last moment they saw each other (in Marseilles, when Isidor, engrossed in a newspaper, wandered on to a Foreign Legion ship instead of joining his wife on the steamer bound for a picturesque Spanish island) up to the present moment of speaking.

I. 2 betäubt: + *dazed;* + *stupefied* (like + *stunned* express the momentary numbing of the senses through shock); (+) *bewildered;* (+) *confused* (these latter two expressions being less colourful as they simply refer to the confusion felt). × *numbed* (although, in addition to its use for purely physical reference, as in "my fingers were numb with cold", 'numbed' can refer to the senses and emotions, as in "her feelings were numbed by the awful news", it is unsuitable in this context, probably because the sensation is so fleeting).

I. 3 einfach: suitable intensifiers here are + *simply* or + *just* if the negation *not ... any more* is used. Note how the two possible positions for the intensifier affect the sentence stress: + *he ·just/·simply ·was ·not.../*+ *he was ·just/·simply ·not....* . *Just* is the more informal intensifier. If the negation is expressed by *no longer,* it is unidiomatic to use *just,* thus: + *he was simply/he simply was no longer....*

II. 3—4 war es ... gewohnt, verheiratet zu sein: take care to use ing-form after *he was accustomed to.../he was used to....* . In the former case only, however, American usage allows the infinitive construction as an alternative, thus: + *he was not accustomed to be....*

II. 3—4 ... verheiratet zu sein: since the reference here is to Isidor's emotional attitude to his family status, it is preferable to use + *to being a married man/to having a wife/to being a husband* rather than (+) *to being married,* which would simply denote his family status legally.

I. 4 und stellte sich: (a) either begin a new sentence, or if you feel that the rather ironic "und" link should be retained, use *"and".* (b) To convey the deliberateness of the action here use + *placed himself;* + *went to stand;* + *took up a position;* + *positioned himself.* × *stood* (might imply unconscious action).

I. 5 die Hände in den Hosentaschen: + *with his hands in his trouser(-) pockets* (no comma required); + *thrusting/digging his hands into his trouser(-)pockets* (more forceful, less casual — adds an element not present in ST).

> "Why didn't you send at least one card?" she asked, whereupon he took his sun-helmet [away] from the bewildered children and, without uttering a [single] word, put it on his own head with the brief sweep he had learned from routine. This [scene] was said to have left an unerasable impression on the children for the rest of their lives — the picture of daddy with his sun-helmet and holster, everything not merely genuine but visibly somewhat worn by use. And when his spouse said: "You know, Isidor, you really shouldn't have done that!" Isidor had had enough of the intimate homecoming; he drew ([once] again with the brief sweep of routine, I fancy) the revolver from his belt and fired three shots right into the middle of the fancily iced cream cake, not yet cut into, which, as one can well imagine, made a considerable mess.

II. 5—6 "Warum ... geschrieben?" An idiomatic expression typical of what a wife would say under such circumstances is required here. Care should be taken to include adequate intensifiers to correspond to the German "nie auch nur". + *"Why couldn't you at least have sent a card?"*/+ *"Why couldn't you have sent just one card?"* (Although no modal is present in ST, the use of "couldn't" here can, I think, be justified on idiomatic grounds.)

II. 6—19: Comprise one single sentence in ST. Although this is undoubtedly a consciously employed device to heighten the dramatic effect, it is extremely difficult, and, for exam purposes at least, probably rather dangerous, to attempt to retain a single sentence in

ET. Various points at which the sentence may be broken lend themselves. An alternative ET might read:

> "Why didn't you send at least one card?" she asked. Thereupon he took his sun-helmet [away] from the bewildered children and, without uttering a [single] word, put it on his own head with the brief sweep he had learned from routine, which [scene] was said to have left an unerasable impression on the children for the rest of their lives — daddy with his sun-helmet and holster, everything not merely genuine but visibly somewhat worn by use. And when ...

l. 6 Darauf: + *At this;* × *on this;* × *upon this;* × *after this* (suggests too great a time lapse before subsequent action).
ll. 6—7 verdutzten: + *baffled;* + *nonplussed;* + *perplexed;* + *startled* (abrupt); + *disconcerted* (less intense); (+) *surprised* (too weak); × *stupefied* (avoid as it can have negative interpretation in this context).
l. 7 setzte: + *placed* (suggests more careful action than put); (+) *donned* (old fashioned but suits this context. However, its use would prescribe omission of the words "on his own head" since "don" = "put on").
l. 8 Schwung: + *sweep* (includes the energy of the movement suggested by ST); × *movement* (too neutral); × *motion* (too neutral); × *swing* (suggests too lengthy a movement, and is especially unsuitable for the context of ll. 15—16, where it needs to be repeated); (+) *flourish* (suggests too elaborate a movement, appropriate perhaps for the donning of the helmet bus less so for the drawing of the revolver (ll. 15—16).
l. 8 mit dem knappen Schwung der Routine: + *with the brief/brisk/snappy/rapid sweep of routine;* + *with the brief sweep he had learned through custom;* + *with a routine military flourish.* (Note zero article with "routine" or "custom".)
ll. 9—10 einen für ... Eindruck: avoid the common error of attempting to render this long pre-modifying attributive phrase in ST by a similar construction in ET. While a single, or series of, adjectives may, of course, premodify the noun, it is impossible to introduce a prepositional phrase in this position. Recourse must be made to post-modifying prepositional or participial phrases, relative clauses, reduced relative clauses, insertions. Thus: ⊗ *a for the rest of their lives unerasable impression.* + *a ... mark/stamp that remained/was to re-*

main with them for the rest of their life/lives; (+) a ... mark that they would never forget during their lifetime. (See also Text A 1, l. 4; ll. 18—19.)

ll. 9—10 unauslöschlich: from a list of possible translations for "auslöschen", such as *erase, blot out, obliterate, efface, cancel, expurgate, expunge, eradicate,* the only verbs that will permit transformation into a viable adjective with negative prefix are *erase* and *eradicate.* × *Ineradicable,* however, is inappropriate for the given context (used mainly in connection with negative and concrete phenomena e.g. habits, diseases, pests etc.). Also: + *indelible.*

l. 10 ... soll ...: + *It is said that this left...;* + *This is supposed to have left...;* × *This should have left* (= it ought to have left but failed to do so!).

l. 10 punctuation: as what succeeds the comma after "soll" is an explanation of what is meant by "Eindruck", English would prefer either a colon or a dash.

ll. 10—11 Papi mit Tropenhelm: addition of possessive determiner optional.

l. 11 alles: × *all* (too few items [only two] listed to justify use of "all". Reference here is to the total impression created).

l. 11 nicht bloß: + *not just;* + *not only.*

l. 11 echt: + *real* (cf. real leather, real life); + *authentic;* × *pure* (cf. pure gold); × *true* (cf. true story; true love).

l. 12 sichtlich: + *obviously;* + *apparently;* + *plainly;* + *evidently.*

l. 12 vom Gebrauche: + *by/through/from use.*

l. 12 die Gattin: + *spouse* (rather old-fashioned, but suits the context and the only possible alternative here to + *wife*).

l. 14 war es ... genug: note past perfect tense obligatory if idiom "to have enough of" is used. Also: + this was enough for Isidor of....

l. 14 der trauten Heimkehr: + *of the/his cosy/sweet return home.*

l. 14 punctuation: what follows the comma after "Heimkehr" expresses the consequence of Isidor's repugnance. Thus a semicolon is preferable. Alternatively a full-stop or colon could be used.

l. 15 zog: × *pulled/*× *took* (unsuitable as they would not indicate the subject's intention to fire the weapon. cf. "he's quick on the draw" = he's quick in drawing a weapon from its holster).

l. 15 mit dem knappen Schwung der Routine: see annotations to ll. 7—8.

l. 16 gab drei Schüsse: + *shot three bullets;* + *sent three shots/ bullets.*

ll. 16—18 in die weiche ... Torte: (a) see notes to ll. 9—10 concerning construction. (b) × *soft cake* might suggest something had gone wrong with the baking of the cake. I have therefore resorted to *cream cake* to render "weiche Torte". Not wishing to indulge in delicious descriptions of British and American baking, let it suffice to say that flans, tarts, and pies do not correspond to what is commonly sold as "Torte". (c) Alteration of the literal translation *decorated with icing* to *fancily iced* conveys more or less the same meaning, at the same time facilitating premodification of the noun, which would, with the presence of a prepositional phrase, otherwise be precluded. Thus post-modification is left open for the remaining two sections. (d) By using a post-modifying insertion to render "bisher noch unberührte", placed between commas, it is possible to accommodate a final relative clause. Also: + *... of the fancily iced cream cake, still untouched/intact, which ... .* ⊗ *...of the still untouched/intact fancily iced cream cake* (impossibly heavy premodification).

ll. 18—19 was ... verursachte: (a) + *and thus made;* + *thus making ...* (b) + *made/caused quite a mess.*

Section B

Text 1: Fachliche Prüfung für das Lehramt an Realschulen, 1976/I

Als junger Mann sagte Churchill einmal: "Es ist besser, die Ereignisse selbst herbeizuführen, als über sie in der Zeitung zu lesen." Er hätte hinzufügen können: "Und noch besser ist es, nachher selbst über sie in der Zeitung zu schrei-
5 ben." Das hat er zwar nicht gesagt, aber er hat es getan.
Er begann, wie er in seinen Jugenderinnerungen erzählt, sein erwachsenes Leben als Offizier und Journalist zugleich. Diese Ausgangsstellung wirkte bestimmend auf seine ganze spätere Geschichtsauffassung hin.
10 Zu jener Zeit, in den neunziger Jahren des vergangenen Jahrhunderts, war es aktiven Offizieren des britischen Heeres noch gestattet, gleichzeitig als Kriegsberichterstatter für Zeitungen zu fungieren. Der junge Churchill machte von dieser Freiheit so ausgiebig und — seinen Vorgesetzten gegenüber —
15 so kritisch Gebrauch, daß schließlich nach dem Sudan-Feldzug dem britischen Berufsheer diese Nebenbeschäftigung vom Kriegsministerium generell ein für allemal verboten wurde.
In Indien war sie noch erlaubt. Churchills erste Kampfhandlung war die Niederwerfung eines Aufstandes von Einheimi-
20 schen an der indischen Nordwestgrenze. Diese blutigen, verlustreichen Kämpfe in unübersichtlichem Gebirgsterrain — nicht unähnlich den Partisanenkämpfen in Jugoslawien während des Zweiten Weltkrieges — waren des Leutnants entscheidendes Erlebnis. Die Berichte, die er an den Londoner "Daily Tele-
25 graph" sandte und wenige Wochen später zu seinem ersten Buch ausgestaltete, zeigen, daß der Vierundzwanzigjährige an der Spitze seiner Truppe und in höchster Lebensgefahr nicht einen Augenblick lang den klaren, präzisen Überblick über die höchst konfuse Gesamtsituation verlor. Ein Freund sagte
30 damals über ihn: "Er kämpfte mit der einen Hand und schrieb mit der anderen. Seine Augen sahen sowohl das, was es sofort zu tun galt, wie das, was später aufzuzeichnen war. Und das war keineswegs dasselbe."

(adapted from Peter de Mendelsohn, **Inselschicksal England,** München, 1965)

"Model" translation(s) and annotations (in sections)

> As a young man Churchill once said: "It's better to bring about events oneself than to read about them in the newspaper." He could have added: "And it's even better to write about them oneself in the newspaper afterwards." He did not say this, it is true, but he did it. He began his adult life, he relates in the memories of his youth, as an officer and a journalist at the same time. This starting point was decisive for the whole of his later conception of history.

l. 1 Als junger Mann: ⊗ *As young man;* (+) *Churchill once said as a young man...;* (+) *Churchill, as a young man, once said....*
l. l sagte Churchill einmal: (a) Simple Past tense obligatory. (b) Word order: × *Churchill said once* (= not twice or thrice).
l. 1 "Es ist besser...": For informal direct speech contracted form of verb may be used, though not obligatory, whereas for main narrative contracted form would be stylistically inappropriate.
ll. 1–2 die Ereignisse: (a) (+) *the events* (inclusion of definite article possible on account of following clause: "than to write about them..."). (b) (+) *happenings;* × *occurrences;* × *incidents* (these nouns all suggest too trivial action for the context).
l. 2 herbeizuführen: (+) *bring ... to pass;* × *to cause;* × *to occasion;* × *to give the occasion for.*
l. 3 Er hätte hinzufügen können: + *He might have added;* × *He might/could have been able to add.*
ll. 3–4 "Und noch besser ist es...": (+) *And it is still better* (reference of "still" ambiguous here — could have temporal meaning).
l. 5 Das hat er zwar nicht gesagt, aber er hat es getan: Simple Past tense obligatory for both verbs.
l. 5 ...zwar...: + *He did not in fact say this but...;* (+) *He did not say this, to be sure, but...* (rather informal).
l. 5 aber er hat es getan: + *but he did so.*
l. 6 Er begann: (a) Simple Past tense obligatory. (b) + *He started [out on] his life...;* + *He embarked on his life...;* (+) *He commenced his life* (sounds rather stilted).
l. 6 wie er in ... erzählt: (a) + *[as] he narrates in...;* × *[as] he tells us in...;* × *[as] he tells in....* (b) Progressive Aspect inappropriate.
l. 6 in seinen Jugenderinnerungen: + *in his memories of his youth;* + *in the/his reminiscences of his youth;* (+) *in the/his memoirs of his*

youth; (+) *in the/his recollections of his youth;* × *in the/his remembrances of his youth;* × *in the/his reminders of his youth.*
ll. 6—7 sein erwachsenes Leben: + *his life as an adult;* (+) *his life as a grown-up* (rather informal for this context).
l. 7 als Offizier und Journalist: indefinite article obligatory: × *as officer . . . .*
l. 7 zugleich: + *at one and the same time.*
ll. 7—8 Diese Ausgangsstellung: (+) *This point of departure;* (+) *This starting position;* ⊗ *This beginning point/position.*
ll. 8—9 wirkte bestimmend auf . . . hin: (a) Simple Past tense obligatory; (b) + *had a decisive influence/effect on . . .;* + *determined . . .;* + *was to determine . . .* ("be to" used to express future destiny from a past point of view is suitable here).
ll. 8—9 seine ganze spätere Geschichtsauffassung: (+) *his whole later conception of history;* × *all of his later conception of history.*

> At that time, in the nineties of the last century, British army officers in active service were still permitted to act as war correspondents on a newspaper as well. Young Churchill made such full and — with regard to his superiors — [such] critical use of this privilege that in the end(,) after the Sudan campaign(,) the War Office placed a general prohibition on this side-line occupation for the British professional army once and for all.

ll. 10—17: All verbs in Simple Past tense.
l. 10 Zu jener Zeit, in den neunziger Jahren des vergangenen Jahrhunderts, . . .: commas obligatory as the phrase between commas stands in apposition to "At that time".
l. 10 in den neunziger Jahren: + *in the final decade:* × *in the ninety years.*
l. 10 vergangenen: (+) *past;* × *previous* (= seen from a past point of view e.g. "Last year we spent our holidays in Spain. The previous year we'd been to Italy."); × *bygone* (cf. "in bygone days/centuries" — more remote).
ll. 11—12 war es . . . Offizieren . . . noch gestattet: + *. . . officers . . . were still allowed to . . .;* + *it was still possible for . . . officers . . . to . . .;* × *it was still permitted/allowed to . . . officers . . . to . . . .*
l. 11 aktiven Offizieren des britischen Heeres: + *active officers in/of the British army.*
l. 12 als Kriegsberichterstatter: (+) *as war reporters.*

l. 12 ... gleichzeitig ...: + ... *at the same time;* + *British army officers were still permitted to act as war correspondents on a newspaper when in active service.*

l. 13 zu fungieren: (+) *to function as;* (+) *to serve as* (mainly used in connection with fulfilling certain responsibilities over a set period of time e.g. to serve in the army; to serve an apprenticeship; to serve time (= to undergo a prison sentence).

l. 13 Der junge Churchill: × *The young Churchill* (only appropriate if "young" is functioning as a defining attribute, in contrast to e.g. "the middle-aged Churchill").

ll. 13—14 von dieser Freiheit: + *of this freedom;* + *of this right;* (+) *of this liberty.*

ll. 13—15 machte ... so ausgiebig ... Gebrauch: + *made such lavish use of;* + *made such abundant use of;* × *made such plentiful use of;* × *made such prolific use of;* × *made such rich use of.*

l. 14 seinen Vorgesetzten gegenüber: + *regarding his superiors;* + *as regards his superiors;* + *with respect to his superiors;* + *concerning his superiors;* + *as concerns his superiors;* + *as far as his superiors were concerned;* + *in relation to his superiors;* × *in the face of his superiors;* × *opposed to his superiors.*

ll. 12—14 so ausgiebig und ... so kritisch Gebrauch: ⊗ *so full and ... critical use* (cf. He was so quick. He ran so quickly. He was such a quick runner. But: He was so quick a runner.)

l. 15 schließlich: + *finally;* + *eventually;* × *at the end* (= of a play, film, road etc.); × *lastly* (= the last thing to be done: firstly, secondly ... lastly).

ll. 16—17 dem britischen Berufsheer ... verboten wurde: + *the British professional army was/were forbidden by the War Office to carry out this side-line occupation once and for all;* ⊗ *it was forbidden ... to the British professional army ...;* (+) *a general ban was placed/imposed by the War Office on [the practice of] this side-line occupation once and for all* (here active construction, with "the War Office" as subject, would be preferable. cf. "model" ET.)

l. 16 diese Nebenbeschäftigung: + *this side-line;* + *this side-line activity;* (+) *this incidental occupation/activity;* (+) *this additional occupation/activity.*

l. 17 ein für allemal: (a) + *once for all;* + *once and for all time.* (b) preferably placed finally for emphasis. Medial position (i.e. immediately before main verb) also possible.

33

In India it was still allowed. Churchill's first engagement in battle was the suppression of a native uprising on the north-west border(s) of India. This bloody strife, involving heavy losses, in strategically difficult mountainous terrain — not unlike the partisan struggles in Yugoslavia during the Second World War — were the crucial experience for the lieutenant.

ll. 18—23: All verbs in Simple Past tense.
ll. 18—19 Kampfhandlung: + *combative action;* (+) *action in battle;* (+) *battle;* (+) *fighting.*
l. 19 die Niederwerfung: + *the crushing of* . . .; + *when he suppressed/crushed/put down* . . .; × *the putting-down of* . . . (very ugly!); × *the overthrowing* (usually in connection with a government; a régime).
l. 19 eines Aufstandes: + *a rebellion;* + *a rising;* + *a revolt;* (+) *an insurrection;* × *a mutiny;* × *a riot.*
ll. 19—20 . . . von Einheimischen: + . . . *of natives.*
l. 20 an der indischen Nordwestgrenze: × *at the north-west border[s] of India* (suggests too precise a location); + *on India's north-west border[s];* (+) *on the Indian north-west border[s].*
ll. 20—21 verlustreichen: (a) post-modifying phrase required here. (b) Place between commas to avoid making following prepositional phrase of place refer to "losses" instead of "strife". Alternatively exchange the positions of these two phrases: (+) *This bloody strife in strategically difficult mountainous terrain involving heavy losses.* (c) + *This bloody strife, incurring heavy losses,* . . .; + *This bloody strife, which incurred/involved heavy losses,* . . .; + *This bloody strife, with heavy losses,* . . .; (+) *This bloody strife, with serious losses,* . . . .
ll. 20—21 Diese ... Kämpfe: + *These battles;* + *These conflicts;* + *These struggles;* × *These fights.* The following alternatives may only be used in singular: + *This fighting;* + *This strife;* (+) *This engagement.*
l. 21 Gebirgsterrain: + *mountain terrain;* + *mountain[ous] country;* × *territory* (usually according to political or social divisions); × *countryside* (cf. *What beautiful countryside we've passed through!*); × *landscape* (cf. *The landscape of this bay is wonderful*).
l. 22 nicht unähnlich den . . .: + *not dissimilar to* . . .; × *like* . . .; × *similar to* . . . (a double negative item is required here to render the same shade of meaning).
ll. 22—23 während des Zweiten Weltkrieges: + *during/in the Second*

World War (usually with capitals, but not obligatory); + *during/in World War II* (here capitals are required).
ll. 23—24 entscheidendes Erlebnis: + *the decisive experience;* × *the deciding experience.*

> The reports [which/that] he submitted to the London Daily Telegraph and some weeks later wrote up as his first book show that the twenty-four-year-old at the head of his troop and in dire danger of his life never for one [single] moment lost his clear, precise grasp of the whole extremely confused situation. A friend said of him at that time: "He fought with one hand and wrote with the other. His eyes saw both what needed doing immediately and what was to be recorded later. And these were by no means the same [things]."

ll. 24—33: tense: All verbs in Simple Past tense (exc. l. 26 "show").
ll. 24—26 ..., die er ... ausgestaltete, ...: a non-defining relative clause; hence (a) no commas; (b) relative pronoun: + *which;* + *that;* + *zero* (accusative case).
l. 25 sandte: + *sent in to;* + *sent to.*
l. 25 und wenige Wochen später: + *not many weeks later/afterwards;* + *a few weeks later/afterwards;* × *few weeks later/afterwards.*
ll. 25—26 zu seinem ersten Buch ausgestaltete: + *wrote up into ...;* (+) *worked up into ...;* (+) *worked up as ...;* (+) *and from which he a few weeks later wrote his first book ...;* (+) *and which a few weeks later formed the basis of his first book.*
l. 26 zeigen: (a) (+) *bear witness/testimony to the fact that;* (+) *point to the fact that;* × *display.* (b) Progressive Aspect inappropriate.
l. 26 der Vierundzwanzigjährige: (+) *the 24-year-old man;* ⊗ *the 24-years-old [man].*
l. 27 in höchster Lebensgefahr: + *in direst danger of [losing] his life;* (+) *in extreme danger of ...;* (+) *in great danger of ... .*
ll. 27—28 nicht einen Augenblick lang: (a) + *never for a [single] moment;* (+) *did not for a moment.* (b) Word order: (+) *did not lose the clear, precise grasp of the extremely confused situation for a single minute.* (With this word order much of the sentence's strength is lost.)
l. 28 Überblick: (+) *view.*
l. 30 Er kämpfte ... und schrieb: use Simple Aspect.
l. 30 mit der einen Hand: (+) *with the one hand.*

I. 31 mit der anderen: (+) *with the other one.*
I. 31 Seine Augen sahen: + *His eyes took in.../registered.../ noticed...;* × *His eyes looked at....*
II. 31—32 sowohl ... wie ...: +*...(what needed doing immediately) as well as....*
I. 31 das, was: × *that which;* ⊗ *that what.*
II. 31—32 das, was es sofort zu tun galt, ...: + *what had to be done immediately;* (+) *what wanted doing immediately* (rather informal); (+) *what was worth doing immediately.*
I. 32 aufzuzeichnen: + *to be written down;* + *to be noted down;* + *to be reported.*
II. 32—33 Und das war keineswegs dasselbe: + *And they were by no means the same [thing];* + *And they/these were not at all the same;* + *And they/these were by no means identical;* × *And those were...* ("those" is mainly used for remoter reference).

Text 2: Fachliche Prüfung für das Lehramt an Realschulen, 1977/II

Aus der britischen Theatergeschichte

Das englische Theater hat sich nur allmählich von dem schweren Schlag erholt, den ihm die Puritaner im 17. Jahrhundert versetzt haben. Die Restauration hätte ein neuer Anfang sein können; aber man zog es vor, französische Stücke zu spielen und
5 Shakespeare dem neuen Geschmack anzupassen. Seine Stücke mußten umgeschrieben werden, so wie er sie geschrieben hätte, wenn er das Glück gehabt hätte, in der 2. Hälfte des 17. Jahrhunderts zu leben. Natürlich wurden auch weiterhin Stücke geschrieben und aufgeführt; aber die englische Literatur
10 wird seitdem vom Roman und von der Dichtung beherrscht. Erst gegen Ende des 19. Jahrhunderts beobachten wir ein Wiederaufleben des englischen Theaters. Einer der Bahnbrecher war Wilde mit seinen Gesellschaftslustspielen. Als neulich eines der Stücke auf unserer Bühne gegeben wurde (es war
15 "Eine Frau ohne Bedeutung"), bemerkte ein Zuschauer, der Dialog sei zwar geistreich und witzig, die Charaktere seien aber recht hölzern.
Die beiden wirklich bedeutenden Dramatiker um die Jahrhundertwende waren zweifellos Shaw und Galsworthy. Shaw griff
20 die sozialen Fragen seiner Zeit auf. Er versuchte, die Dinge zu zeigen, wie sie in Wirklichkeit waren, frei von jedem gefühlsmäßigen Herkommen. Mit seinem irischen Witz bekämpfte er das, was man "cant" nennt. In "Caesar und Cleopatra" wandte er sich gegen die Romantik Shakespeares, in "Saint
25 Joan" gegen die idealistische Geschichtsauffassung Schillers; in "Man and Superman" entwickelte er im Anschluß an Bergson seine Theorie von der "Lebenskraft". Auch Galsworthy rang mit sozialen Fragen. In "Justice" wird Falder von der blinden Justiz vernichtet; in "The Silver Box" wird ein arbeits-
30 loser Arbeiter wegen eines geringfügigen Diebstahls zu einem halben Jahr Gefängnis verurteilt, während der Sohn eines einflußreichen Abgeordneten wegen desselben Vergehens straffrei ausgeht; in "Loyalties" muß sich ein Außenseiter, ein Jude, sein Recht gegen den vereinten Widerstand der

35 Gesellschaft erkämpfen. Aber Galsworthy wollte, daß wir
beide Seiten sehen sollten. Daher haben seine Stücke keinen
richtigen Schluß; sie sollen uns zum Nachdenken anregen. Sie
sind ein leidenschaftliches Eintreten für menschliches Mitgefühl und gegenseitiges Verstehen. Man kann die beiden nicht
40 vergleichen; wenn man es versuchte, wäre man ungerecht. Jeder
von ihnen hat auf seine Art Bleibendes geschaffen.

Particular attention should be paid in the translation of this text to the choice between Simple Past and Present Perfect tenses.

"Model" translation(s) and annotations (in sections)

From the History of the British Theatre

> The British theatre has only gradually recovered from the heavy blow [that/which it was] dealt by the Puritans in the seventeenth century. The Restoration could have been a new beginning but preference was given to performing French plays and to adapting Shakespeare to the new taste. His plays had to be rewritten(,) the way he would have written them if he had been lucky enough to live in the second half of the seventeenth century. Other plays continued, of course, to be written and put on the stage; but English literature has, since that time, been dominated by the novel and poetry.

l. 1 das englische Theater: probably imprecise use of "englisch" (very frequent in German) to refer to "British". (see also notes, text A 2, l. 1.)
ll. 1—2 hat sich ... erholt: (a) reference is made here to a time-span reaching from the 17th century up to present times; hence Present Perfect obligatory. (b) (+) *has recuperated from;* × *has recovered itself;* × *has recuperated itself.*
ll. 1—2 von dem ... Schlag ..., den ...: a defining relative clause; thus (a) no comma; (b) relative pronoun: + *that*/+ *which*/+ *zero* (accusative case).
l. 2 Schlag: × *hit;* × *knock.*
ll. 1—2 von dem schweren Schlag: + *from the severe*/+ *serious*/+ *grievous blow;* (+) *from the weighty blow;* × *from the hard*/× *strong blow.*

l. 2 versetzt haben: (a) Tense: Simple Past ("in the seventeenth century"); (b) +... *it received;* × ... *it was given.*
l. 3 Die Restauration: (a) definite article obligatory; (b) watch the spelling of "Restoration".
ll. 3—4 hätte ... sein können: + *could have meant;* + *could have marked;* + *could have brought.*
l. 3 ein neuer Anfang: × *a new start* (unsuitable for this context. cf. "After leaving prison he made a new start in life").
l. 4 aber man zog es vor: (+) *but it was preferred to (+ inf.);* (+) *but they preferred to...;* × *but one preferred to...;* × *but people preferred to.* Use Simple Past.
l. 4 Stücke: × *pieces.*
l. 4 zu spielen: + *to producing;* + *to staging;* + *to putting on;* (+) *to acting;* × *to playing.* Alternatively use infinitive form if one of the structures suggested in annotations l. 4 is used.
l. 5 anzupassen: (a) take care: use infinitive or -ing form as in previous structure. (b) × *to adjust[ing]* (cf. to adjust the tv, the volume, the focus of the camera, one's speed/driving style etc.).
l. 6 so wie er sie geschrieben hätte: + *in the way he would have written them;* + *as he would have written them;* × *like he would have written them.*
l. 7 wenn er das Glück gehabt hätte: + *if he had had the good fortune to...;* + *if he had been fortunate enough to...;* × *if he had had the luck to... .*
l. 8 zu leben: + *to be living;* (+) *to be alive.*
l. 9 aufgeführt: + *performed;* + *staged;* + *presented on the stage;* + *produced.*
ll. 9—10 die englische Literatur: × *the English literature.*
l. 10 wird ... beherrscht: Present Perfect Simple required in ET. × *is dominated... .*
ll. 9—10 aber ... beherrscht: + *but [ever] since that time/* + *[ever] since then/* + *ever since English literature has been dominated by...;* (+) *but English literature has been dominated by the novel and poetry ever since that time* (inferior style as too great focus is thus imparted to the time adverbial).
l. 10 vom Roman und von der Dichtung: (+) *by fiction and poetry;* × *by the novel and the poetry;* × *by the novel and the poem.*

> Not until the close of the nineteenth century can a revival of the British theatre be observed. One of the pioneers was Wilde with his social comedies. When one of the plays was performed recently on our stage (namely "A Woman of No Importance") a member of the audience remarked that the dialogue was indeed ingenious and witty, but the characters were downright awkward.

I. 11 Erst...: + *Not before;* × *only.*
I. 11 gegen Ende des 19. Jahrhunderts: + *towards the close/end of the 19th century.*
II. 11—12 Erst gegen Ende ... des englischen Theaters: Inversion required following initial placement (for emphasis) of negative or restrictive phrase: ⊗ *Not until the close of the 19th century a revival can be observed.* Alternatively a cleft construction (see UGE, chap. 14) could be used: + *It is/was not until the close of the 19th century that a revival of the British theatre can/could be observed.* × *It is/was not until the close of the 19th century when a revival ... .*
I. 11 beobachten wir: Impersonal passive construction preferable: see "model" ET. (+) *... do we observe.*
II. 13—14 Als neulich eines der Stücke auf unserer Bühne gegeben wurde: Word order: + *When, recently, one of the plays ...;* + *When one of the plays was recently performed.* (Note: Simple Past tense required here ["recently" = a short time ago].)
I. 15 bemerkte: + *commented;* + *observed;* × *realised;* × *noticed* (here a verbal statement is made). Note: Simple Past tense obligatory.
II. 15—17 der Dialog sei ... recht hölzern: Verbs in indirect speech require Simple Past tense here (dependent on introductory verb in Simple Past tense).
I. 16 ... zwar ...: + *... the dialogue was certainly ingenious and witty, but ...;* + *... the dialogue might be ingenious and witty but ...;* + *even if/though the dialogue was ingenious and witty, the characters ...;* (+) *despite the fact that the dialogue was ingenious and witty, the characters ...* (rather wordy).
I. 16 geistreich: + *witty;* (+) *clever.*
I. 16 witzig: (+) *funny.*
I. 17 hölzern: + *stiff;* + *wooden;* + *artificial;* + *unnatural;* (+) *clumsy.*
I. 17 recht: + *really;* + *quite;* + *very;* + *extremely;* × *rather;* × *pretty* (latter two too weak); × *right* (too informal).

The two dramatists of real significance at the turn of the century were undoubtedly Shaw and Galsworthy. Shaw took up the social questions of his age. He tried to portray things as they really were, free of any emotional tradition. With his Irish wit he attacked what is called "cant". In "Caesar and Cleopatra" he took a stand against Shakespeare's romanticism, in "Saint Joan" against Schiller's idealistic conception of history; in "Man and Superman" he developed, in the manner of Bergson, his theory of "life energy".

l. 18 Die beiden wirklich bedeutenden Dramatiker: + *the two really important/significant/great dramatists;* × *the two real great dramatists* ("wirklich" is an adverb here, modifying "bedeutenden"!).
l. 19 waren: Simple Past tense obligatory here ("um die Jahrhundertwende"). Use same tense to l. 28 "rang".
l. 19 zweifellos: + *without doubt;* + *indubitably;* (+) *unquestionably.*
l. 20 seiner Zeit: + *of his times;* × *of his time.*
l. 20 Er versuchte...: + *He endeavoured to...;* + *He strove to...;* (+) *He attempted to....*
ll. 20—21 die Dinge zu zeigen: × *to show the things* (not specifically identified; thus general reference with zero article!).
l. 21 wie sie in Wirklichkeit waren: + *as they were in reality;* × *like they really were.*
l. 22 Witz: + *with his Irish [sense of] humour.*
l. 22 bekämpfte: + *he opposed;* (+) *he fought against;* (+) *he stood up against;* (+) *he did battle with.*
l. 23 ...das, was...: × *...that which;* ⊗ *...that what....*
l. 23 was man "cant" nennt: (+) *what people call "cant".*
l. 25 Geschichtsauffassung: + *concept of history.*
ll. 26—27 im Anschluß an Bergson: + *..., in the tradition of Bergson, ...;* + *..., following on from Bergson, ...;* × *in continuation of Bergson.*
l. 27 "Lebenskraft": + *"vital energy";* + *vitality;* + *vigour;* (+) *energy for life.*

Galsworthy also wrestled with social issues. In "Justice" Falder is destroyed by blind justice; in "The Silver Box" an unemployed labourer is sentenced to half a year's imprisonment for a petty theft(,) while the son of an influential member of parliament is acquitted of the [very] same offence; in "Loyalties" an outsider, a Jew, has to fight for his rights against the united opposition of society.

ll. 27—28 Auch Galsworthy rang...: + *Galsworthy, too, wrestled...* (Note: commas obligatory as "too" — generally placed finally — here takes up an unusual position); (+) *Galsworthy wrestled with social issues too* (stylistically preferable to end on "social issues"); (+) *Even Galsworthy wrestled...;* × *Galsworthy wrestled also...* ("also" generally placed medially); × *Also Galsworthy wrestled....*
l. 28 rang mit...: + *grappled with...;* (+) *struggled with...;* (+) *struggled to cope with....*
ll. 28—29 von der blinden Justiz: × *by the blind justice* (zero article with abstract noun used with general reference); × *by the blind judicial system* (meaning changed!).
l. 30 Arbeiter: + *worker;* + *workman.*
ll. 30—31 wird zu einem halben Jahr Gefängnis verurteilt: + *is sentenced to six months' imprisonment;* × *is sentenced to half a year of imprisonment;* (+) *is condemned to...* (cf. condemned/sentenced to death; condemned/sentenced to life imprisonment; sentenced to a year's imprisonment).
l. 30 wegen eines geringfügigen Diebstahls: (a) (+) *on account of a petty theft;* (+) *because of a petty theft;* × *due to a petty theft.* (b) +...*a minor theft;* (+) ...*an insignificant theft;* × ...*an unimportant theft.*
l. 31 während: + *whereas.*
ll. 32—33 wegen desselben Vergehens straffrei ausgeht: + *gets away with the same offence;* + *is let off for the same offence;* + *gets off scotfree with/for the same offence* (these three alternatives more informal than the "model" ET).
ll. 34—35 sein Recht erkämpfen: × *to fight for his right.*
ll. 34—35 der Gesellschaft: zero article here, where the reference is general, non-specific.

> But Galsworthy wanted us to see both sides. That is why his plays have no proper ending [to them]; they are intended to stimulate the reader to think. They are a passionate appeal for human sympathy and mutual understanding. The two cannot be compared; to try to do so would be unfair. Each of them, in his [own] way, has created something which will endure.

ll. 35—36 Aber Galsworthy wollte, daß wir beide Seiten sehen sollten: ⊗ *But G. wanted that we see/should see both sides.*
l. 36 Daher: + *This is why...;* + *For this reason...;* (+) *For that*

reason... (Since reference is to immediately preceding sentence "that" seems somewhat remote.) (+) *His plays, therefore, have* ....
l. 37 richtigen: + *real;* + *actual.*
l. 37 Schluß: + *conclusion;* × *end* (of course, the play does have a concrete beginning and an end).
l. 37 sie sollen uns zum Nachdenken anregen: (a) + *he intends them to stimulate the reader to think;* (+) *they should stimulate the reader to think;* (b) + *they are intended to make the reader think;* + *they are intended to stimulate the reader's thoughts;* + *they are intended to stimulate/promote thought/reflection on the part of the reader.*
l. 38 leidenschaftliches: + *impassioned;* + *vehement.*
l. 38 Eintreten: + *intercession for ...;* + *engagement for ....*
ll. 38—39 Mitgefühl: + *compassion;* (+) *pity.*
ll. 39—40 Man kann die beiden nicht vergleichen: Preferably use an impersonal passive construction. ⊗ *Both cannot be compared;* ⊗ *The both ....*
l. 40 wenn man es versuchte, wäre man ungerecht: (+) *if one tried to do so one would be unfair/unjust.* (Repetition of "one" unfavourable.)
l. 41 tense: Present Perfect tense most likely here. Simple Past tense also acceptable.
l. 41 Bleibendes: + *something which will last;* (+) *something lasting/ enduring;* × *something which lasts/endures.*

Text 3: Fachliche Prüfung für das Lehramt an Realschulen, 1978/I

Vom Urlaub zurück

Wenn einer vom Urlaub zurückkommt, dann ist er noch gar nicht da, wenn er auch schon da ist. "Na, wie war's?" sagen die andern. "Sie sehn aber schön erholt aus! Gutes Wetter gehabt?" Darauf fängt er an zu erzählen. Wenn er aber Ohren hat zu
5 hören, so merkt er, daß die Frage eigentlich mehr gesellschaftlicher Natur war — so genau wollen es die andern gar nicht wissen.
Wenn einer vom Urlaub zurückgekehrt ist, gehört er in den ersten beiden Tagen noch nicht so recht zum Betrieb. Wäh-
10 rend seiner Abwesenheit haben sich vielerlei kleine Sachen ereignet, von denen er natürlich nicht unterrichtet ist, und so versteht er manche Anspielungen nicht, der Betrieb geht über den Kopf des Ex-Urlaubers hinweg: die andern wissen alles, er weiß nur die Hälfte. Die da werfen sich die Bälle
15 zu — er fängt sie nicht.
In seinen Gesprächen flackert immer noch der Urlaub auf. Einmal denkt er: "Heute vor acht Tagen . . .", aber da klingelt das Telefon, und die Erinnerung zerstiebt. Dann kommt wieder einer vorbei, stellt die üblichen Fragen, und er antwortet.
20 "Danke — nur viel zu kurz! So — Sie gehen jetzt auch auf Urlaub?" Aber das interessiert wieder den ehemaligen Urlauber nicht mehr.
In diesen ersten Tagen geht die Arbeit eigentlich nicht leichter als vor dem Urlaub; sie geht eher etwas schwerer
25 vonstatten. Die Lungen sind noch voll frischer Luft, der Körper hat noch den Rhythmus des Schwimmens und des Laufens in sich, die Haut fühlt sich in den Stadtkleidern noch nicht wohl, und der Hals nicht im Kragen. Das Auge sieht zum Hof hinaus; wenn man den Kopf dreht, kann man ein Stückchen
30 blauen Himmel sehen. Übrigens ist er heute nicht blau, es regnet. Aber der Regen im Freien, das war doch ganz etwas anderes.
Das dauert gut und gern seine drei, vier Tage. Dann haben sich die andern an den Zurückgekehrten gewöhnt; er gehört nun
35 schon wieder dazu, er ist da, er erlebt es alles mit, nichts

kittet so aneinander wie gemeinschaftliches Arbeits-Erlebnis. Das kommt gleich nach der Liebe und nach der Gottbehüte Verwandtschaft.

Nach sechs Tagen fragt ihn kein Mensch mehr nach dem Urlaub, nun kommen auch die letzten Sommerurlauber zurück, alle sind wieder da und fangen ganz langsam an, sich auf den nächsten Urlaub zu freuen.

Aus: Kurt Tucholsky, Kleines Lesebuch. München 1977 (DTV)

Particular difficulties in this text are the tenses (esp. Present Perfect: Simple Past) and choice of aspect.

"Model" translation(s) and annotations (in sections)

Back from the holidays

> When a person comes back from his holiday[s] he is not yet back at all even though he actually already is. "Well, what was it like?" the others say. "You really look wonderfully rested! Did you have good weather?" At this he starts relating his adventures. But if he has ears to hear, he will notice that the question was in fact more a sociable one — the others are not really interested in hearing all the details.

Title: + Back from holiday; + Back from [the] vacation; × Back from holidays.

l. 1 einer: + someone/somebody; × one (it would sound too stilted to use this pronoun throughout the text); × you (it would sound too personal to use this pronoun throughout the text). Possessive determiner following: a person = + his. (In other formal contexts, e.g. a public notice, it is more correct to use the alternative possessive determiner "his or her" e.g. "Will the person who has lost his or her wallet please report to the secretariat."); someone/somebody = + his (in certain contexts where female numbers clearly dominate, it may be appropriate to use "her").

l. 1 Wenn: + Whenever; × If.

l. 1 vom Urlaub zurückkommt: + comes back from holiday; + returns from holiday/his holiday[s]/his vacation; × is returning/× is coming back.

ll. 1—2 dann ist er noch gar nicht da: (a) (+) *then he is not yet back at all.* (ET reads more fluently without "then".) (b) intensifier to render "noch gar nicht": + ... *not yet back at all;* (+) ... *by no means back yet.* (c) (+) *he is not there at all;* + ... *still not back at all.*
l. 2 wenn ... auch: + *even if;* × *if ... also.*
l. 2 wenn er auch schon da ist: + *even though/if he in fact already is [back].* (Note: for contrastive focus "is" is stressed; thus "already" is placed before the verb. cf. "He is already back" [verb unstressed].)
l. 2 "Na, wie war's?": + *Well,/* + *Hey, how was it?* + *Well, how was it then?* ⊗ *Well, how was it like?*
ll. 2—3 sagen die anderen: + *the others ask.* (+) *say/ask the others* (more literary/old-fashioned style).
l. 3 Sie sehen aber schön erholt aus!: + *You're really looking wonderfully rested/*(+) *wonderfully well;* + *You're really looking much better/* (+) *well!* (English idiom here permits use of either Simple or Progressive aspect with "look". If Progressive aspect is used, employ contracted form (informal spoken style). + *you do look well* (with "do" stressed). × *But you look very well.*
l. 3 Gutes Wetter gehabt?: + *Was the weather good?* (Present Perfect would be inappropriate here as the holidaymaker is no longer at the beach but back in his grey office!) × *Was the weather fine?* ("fine" used in connection with the weather = [simply] not raining).
l. 4 Darauf: + *In reply;* + *Then;* (+) *Upon this* (sounds stilted); (+) *Thereupon* (rather too formal here); × *On this.*
l. 4 fängt er an zu erzählen: + *he begins his account;* + *he starts/ begins telling them about it all;* + *he starts/begins to tell them about it all;* × *he is starting ...;* (+) ... *to recount/recounting his adventures;* (+) ... *to talk/talking;* (+) ... *to tell them/telling them;* ⊗ ... *to tell/ telling;* × ... *to relate/relating [to them];* × ... *to recount/recounting* (in the latter two cases direct object required).
ll. 4—5 Wenn er aber Ohren hat zu hören: + *But if he has sensitive ears;* (+) *But if he pricks up his ears* (= die Ohren spitzen); × *But if he uses his ears* (too informal here). "Model" ET is preferable as it is the accepted ET of the biblical phrase used in ST.
l. 5 so merkt er: + *[then] he will notice/he notices* (ET reads more fluently without "then"). + *he will realise/he realises;* × *he is noticing;* × *he will remark* (= comment); × *so he will notice ....*
ll. 5—6 daß die Frage mehr gesellschaftlicher Natur war: + *that the*

question was really/in fact more of a social nature ... (Note: no comma before "that"-clause.)

ll. 6—7 so genau wollen es die andern gar nicht wissen: + *the others do not want to hear about it in such detail at all;* + *the others do not really want to know the exact details;* + *the others do not really want to know so exactly.*

> When a person has returned from his holidays he does not, in the first two days, really yet belong to the working staff. During his absence many a little thing has happened(,) of which he, of course, is not informed(,) and thus he fails to understand many allusions. The activities of the staff pass right over the ex-holidaymaker's head: the others know everything; he only knows [the] half. They exchange banter — he does not understand it.

l. 8 gehört: Simple Present obligatory ("Belong" is one of the group of verbs not normally used in Progressive aspect).

ll. 8—9 word order: By using an insertion for the time adverbial it is possible to avoid final placement, thus reserving the position of information focus for the ET of "zum Betrieb". (see UGE, chap. 14.)

l. 9 Betrieb: the meaning here is rather different from that in l. 12 (See "model" translation and note to l. 12). (+) *the office* (depends on place of work).

ll. 9—10 Während seiner Abwesenheit: + *In his absence;* + *while he was absent/away;* + *While he has been absent/away.*

ll. 10—11 haben sich ... ereignet: + *happened* (Present Perfect Simple or Simple Past appropriate, but use the same tense [if one was used at all] as for "während seiner Abwesenheit"). × *has been happening* (Progr. incompatible with sing. subject); × *was happening.*

l. 10 vielerlei kleine Sachen: (+) *many little things.*

l. 11 von denen er natürlich nicht unterrichtet ist: (a) This relative clause can be interpreted as either defining (without commas) or non-defining (with commas). (b) +... *(,) which he, of course, is not informed of/about(,)* ... (less formal word order). (c) +...*(,) of which he is, of course, uninformed (,)* ...; +...*(,) of which he, of course, has no idea (,)* ...; (+) ...*(,) of which, naturally, he has not been told (,)* ... .

ll. 11—12 und so ...: + *and therefore* ...; + *and so* ... (less formal).

l. 12 versteht er ... nicht: Simple Aspect obligatory. ("understand"/

47

"comprehend" belong to the group of verbs not normally used in the Progressive Aspect.)
l. 12 manche Anspielungen: (a) + *some/many allusions;* + *many an allusion.* (b) + ... *references;* + ... *implications;* × *insinuations* (too negative here).
l. 12 der Betrieb: + *[the] office work;* + *the work of the office;* + *office proceedings;* × *[the] office organisation;* × *the working staff.*
ll. 12–13 geht über den Kopf des Ex-Urlaubers hinweg: + *goes [right] over the ex-holidaymaker's head*/(+) *the head of the ex-holidaymaker* (former alternative preferable as less focus is lent to given information ("ex-holidaymaker"). (See UGE, chap. 14.)
l. 14 punctuation: ET requires a semi-colon, not a comma, here.
ll. 14–15 Die da werfen sich die Bälle zu – er fängt sie nicht: (a) both verbs should be in Simple Aspect. (b) There is no corresponding idiom in English to that used in ST. A literal translation, though understandable from the context, would thus be rather unidiomatic: (+) *They throw balls to each other – he does not catch them.* An alternative non-literal translation: + *They give each other cues – he does not understand them.*

> In his conversations the topic "holiday" still keeps coming up. Once he thinks: "A week ago today...", but then the telephone rings and the memory turns to dust. Then someone else comes along, asks the usual questions and he answers: "All right, thanks – but much too short! Well – and you're going on holiday now, aren't you?" But this is something the former holidaymaker is no longer interested in.

l. 16 flackert ... auf: × *flares up;* × *blazes up.* (Although these two verbs are used to describe flames, both suggest too violent or dramatic intensity for this context. cf. Trouble has flared up in Northern Ireland again recently.)
l. 16 ... flackert immer noch der Urlaub auf: + *still comes up;* × *is still coming up;* + *still crops up* (fairly colloquial but appropriate for this context).
ll. 16–22: Aspect: Simple Present should be used throughout this section (sequence of events).
l. 18 die Erinnerung: + *the remembrance;* × *the reminder* (cf. "In today's post I received a reminder to pay my phone bill."); × *the*

memorial (cf. "We visited the war memorial in the Haymarket yesterday.").
l. 18 zerstiebt: + *shatters* (Although the image of dust is lost with the use of this verb, the intensity of fragmentation, expressed in ST by the prefix "zer-", is conveyed).
ll. 18—19 Dann kommt wieder einer vorbei: + *Then someone else comes by/drops in/drops by/pops in/pops by* ("pop" and "drop" more informal than "come" here).
l. 20 "Danke...": In answer to the "usual questions" (as exemplified in ll. 2—3) he would not simply say "Thanks", but rather + *"Yes, thanks"/*+ *"All right, thanks"/*+ *"OK, thanks"* or, showing greater enthusiasm than ST perhaps, (+) *"Great, thanks"/*(+) *"Fine, thanks".*
ll. 20—21 — Sie gehen jetzt auch auf Urlaub?: + *...and you're going to take your holiday[s]/a holiday now, aren't you?* + *...and are you going on holiday now?* + *...and are you going to go on holiday now?* + *...and are you taking/going to take your holiday now?*
ll. 21—22 Aber das interessiert wieder den ehemaligen Urlauber nicht mehr: + *But this no longer interests the former holidaymaker.*

> During these first few days work is actually no easier than [it was] before the holiday; it rather proceeds somewhat more laboriously. The lungs are still full of fresh air, the body is still adapted to the rhythm of swimming and running, the skin does not yet feel comfortable in city clothes, nor does the neck in the collar. Your gaze wanders [out on] to the yard; if you turn your head, you can catch a glimpse of a tiny patch of blue sky. By the way, the sky is not blue today; it is raining. But [the] rain [outside] in the open [air] — that was something quite different.

l. 23 In diesen ersten Tagen: + *In these first [few] days;* (+) *On these first [few] days.*
l. 23 die Arbeit: × *the work.*
ll. 23—24 geht ... eigentlich nicht leichter: + *is not really [any] easier.*
ll. 24—25 sie geht eher etwas schwerer vonstatten: + *it rather progresses somewhat more laboriously;* + *on the contrary it proceeds/progresses with somewhat greater difficulty.* Use Simple Aspect.
ll. 25—27 der Körper hat noch den Rhythmus ... in sich: + *the body still has in it the rhythm...* (In this way the stylistically inferior final placement of "in it" can be avoided.)
ll. 27—28 die Haut fühlt sich ... noch nicht wohl: (+) *the skin does not*

yet feel good...; × *the skin does not yet feel well...* (Simple Aspect should be used.)
l. 27 in den Stadtkleidern: × *in the city clothes.*
ll. 25—28 Die Lungen ... Kragen: alternatively, change the sentence round: + *Fresh air still fills the lungs, the rhythm of swimming and running still controls the body, the city clothes still feel uncomfortable on the skin, as does the collar around the neck.*
ll. 29—30 kann man ... sehen: + *you can see...;* + *you can catch sight of...;* (+) *you can espy...* (rather literary for the informal style of ST).
l. 30 Übrigens: + *Actually;* + *In fact;* × *Besides* (inappropriate here as it is not an addition but rather a contrast that is expressed).
ll. 30—31 ... ist er heute nicht blau, es regnet: (a) × *it is not blue today; it is raining.* (Owing to the use of "it" in the subsequent phrase, ET requires substitution of a noun for the first pronoun in ST.) (b) Note: English requires the use of a semi-colon here. (See also l. 35.)

> This [state] easily goes on for three or four days. Then the others have grown accustomed to the returnee; now he once again belongs to them, he is back, he experiences everything at first hand; nothing binds people to each other so much as a common work experience. It is next to love and the — God forbid — relatives.

l. 33 Das dauert: + *This [state] lasts;* (+) *... endures;* × *... takes;* × *... is lasting.*
ll. 33—34 Dann haben sich die andern an ... gewöhnt: + *Then/By then the others have got used/got accustomed to...;* (+) *Then the others have accustomed themselves to....*
l. 34 den Zurückgekehrten: (+) *their returned work-mate/fellow-worker* (very wordy).
l. 35 er erlebt es alles mit: (a) (+) *he gets to know everything;* (+) *he is experiencing everything at first hand.* (b) AmE permits omission of preposition "at": + *first hand.*
ll. 35—36 nichts kittet so aneinander wie...: + *Nothing forms quite such a bond between people as...;* + *Nothing binds people to each other as fast as.../more than...;* + *Nothing glues ...* (not fig.); × *Nothing cements...* (cf. "This experience together has cemented the relationship".) Use Simple Aspect here!
l. 37 Gottbehüte: here the ST is very ironical, with the meaning "the damned relatives". To translate: × *and the relatives — God bless them*

would be to risk the loss of the ironical, and therefore substitution of a purely positive, interpretation.

> Six days later nobody else enquires about his holiday; now the last summer holidaymakers also return; everyone is back again and begins(,) very slowly(,) to look forward to the next holiday.

l. 39 Nach sechs Tagen: + *After six days.*
l. 39 fragt ihn ... nach: + *asks him about...;* ⊗ *enquires him about....*
ll. 40—41 alle sind ... und fangen ... an ...: Note: "everyone" followed by a 3rd person singular verb!
l. 41 und fangen ganz langsam an: + *and very slowly begins...;* (+) *and very slowly starts...* (more informal than "begins").
ll. 41—42 sich ... zu freuen: + *to look/*+ *looking forward to...* (both forms possible with both "to begin" and "to start").
ll. 39—42 Aspect: preferably use Simple Present for all the verbs in this section. Use of the Progressive Aspect could, however, be justified in l. 40: + *are returning* and/or l. 41: + *is beginning,* in both of which cases a gradual process or development would thus be implied.

Section C

Text 1: Wissenschaftliche Prüfung für das Lehramt an den Gymnasien, 1975/II

Kingsley Amis

Amis wurde in einem Londoner Vorort als Sohn eines Büroangestellten geboren. Durch ein Stipendium fand er Aufnahme in eine gute Londoner Tagesschule. Nach seiner Schulzeit und einer unausgegorenen marxistischen Phase, die er für
5   seine Generation als fast verbindlich erachtet, trat er in die Armee ein und nahm als Nachrichtenoffizier am Krieg teil. Ein weiteres Stipendium verschaffte ihm Einlaß in eines der weniger snobistischen Studienkollegs, wo er Philip Larkin und John Wain kennenlernte. Die Freundschaft, die
10 ihn mit beiden verband, hinterließ ihre Spuren im Werk aller drei Schriftsteller. Sie kamen wie der größte Teil der übrigen College-Insassen aus vergleichbaren sozialen Verhältnissen und teilten dieselben Probleme: die Verwirrung über die Fortdauer des akademischen Leerlaufs, der gelehr-
15 samen Unverbindlichkeit und Selbstbespiegelung, über Autoritätsanmaßung, Traditionsgläubigkeit und Kulturphilistertum. Amis fühlte sich nach seinen Worten wohl am St John's College; nicht nur, weil er dort Gleichgesinnte traf, sondern auch, weil die meisten seiner Kommilitonen intelligent
20 und fleißig waren und von dem Kult des Versagens, wie er eine Dekade später Mode wurde, nichts wissen wollten. Obwohl die Hauptgestalt seines ersten Erfolgsromanes — Jim Dixon — auch autobiographische Züge trägt, ist der Versuch, Amis mit Dixon gleichzusetzen oder letzteren in einen
25 positiven Helden umzumünzen, ebenso fragwürdig wie die manchmal geäußerte Behauptung, Amis habe nichts weiter Bemerkenswertes zu sagen. Amis bemerkt über Jim Dixon, dieser habe während seines bisherigen Lebens stets gesehen, wie Macht und Stellung denen zufielen, die weniger durch ihre
30 Fähigkeiten als durch ihre glatten Manieren, ihren 'gebildeten' Tonfall und durch den Einfluß hervortraten, den sie

oder ihre Väter ausüben konnten. Dieser neue Typus eines
Helden ist ein etwas 'vergammelter' junger Mann, der verwirrt, aber nicht eigentlich beeindruckt ist von einer Gesell-
35 schaftshierarchie, die sich als selbstverständlich ausgibt, von einer führenden Schicht, die angemaßte Vorrechte
geltend macht.
Ein völlig ablehnendes Urteil fällt 1955 der damals über
80jährige Somerset Maugham. Zwar ist auch er von Amis'
40 schriftstellerischem Talent überzeugt, hält dessen Gestalten
jedoch für Abschaum. Sie gingen nicht auf die Universität,
um sich Kultur anzueignen, sondern um eine Stellung zu bekommen; hätten sie erst eine, würden sie darin verlottern. Sie
hätten keine Manieren und seien unfähig, mit Schwierigkeiten
45 im gesellschaftlichen Bereich fertig zu werden. Maugham
drückt seine Befriedigung darüber aus, nicht mehr zu leben,
wenn diese Generation erst einmal im Parlament vertreten
sein werde.

Englische Literatur der Gegenwart in Einzeldarstellungen, hrsg. von
H. Drescher

Particular difficulties in this text are presented by the choice of tenses,
especially to render indirect speech; relative clauses; abstract nouns;
the use of the definite article.

"Model" translation(s) and annotations (in sections)

Kingsley Amis

> Amis was born in a London suburb as [the] son of a clerk. With the
> aid of a scholarship he gained admission to a reputable London
> day school. After leaving school and after an unripe Marxist phase,
> which for his generation he considers [as] almost essential, he
> joined the army and served in the war as a signals officer.

**II. 1—2 Amis wurde in einem Londoner Vorort als Sohn eines Büro-
angestellten geboren:** + *Amis was born the son of a clerk in a London
suburb.* (Note: modern idiom prefers to omit "as" in this construction.
In this context, however, this involves assigning place adjunct to final
position, which gives the adjunct undue emphasis (see UGE chap. 14).

II. 1—2 eines Büroangestellten: (+) *of an office employee;* × *of an employee* (= anyone who works, in whatever capacity, for an employer).
I. 2 Durch ein Stipendium: (a) + *By means of a scholarship/* (+) *Through a scholarship/*(+) *By a scholarship;* (b) × *grant* (mainly for university or higher education and usually provided by state; *scholarship* generally awarded by sponsor on merit).
I. 2 fand er Aufnahme: + *he obtained admission to;* + *he was admitted to;* + *he was accepted by;* (+) *he gained/obtained entrance to;* × *he gained/obtained entry to* (= managed to enter the building).
I. 2 Durch ein Stipendium fand er Aufnahme: + *He won a scholarship to;* + *A scholarship enabled him to attend;* + *A scholarship gained/procured him admission to.*
I. 3 in eine gute Londoner Tagesschule: + *to a good London day school* (= not a boarding school); + *to a good day school in London.*
I. 3 Nach seiner Schulzeit: + *After finishing school;* + *When/After his schooldays were over;* (+) *After his time at school;* × *After his school time.*
I. 4 und einer unausgegorenen marxistischen Phase: (a) + *and [after] an unripe Marxist phase/period;* + *and [after] an unripe period/phase of Marxism;* × *and [after] a phase/period of unripe Marxism* (wrong noun is modified here); (b) **unausgegorenen:** lit. = the process of fermentation is cut short, not brought to an end. × *Unfermented* is, however, unsuitable here (fig. = not stirred up; not agitated). + *unfulfilled;* (+) *immature* (could reflect negatively on "Marxist phase"); (+) *unreflected.*
II. 4—5 ..., die er für seine Generation als fast verbindlich erachtet: non-defining relative clause; thus commas obligatory. + *..., which for his generation he holds to be almost essential, ...;* + *..., which he considers/holds to be almost essential for his generation, ...* .
I. 5 fast verbindlich: + *almost obligatory/mandatory/compulsory/indispensable;* × *nearly essential/obligatory* etc. ("Nearly" only used with reference to specifically measurable point or degree. "Almost" can be used in latter case and also for vaguer reference. e.g. We've + *nearly/*+ *almost arrived*. It's + *nearly/*+ *almost noon*. He's + *nearly/*+ *almost finished*. She + *nearly/*+ *almost dropped the tray*. But: He was × *nearly/*+ *almost happy*. His death can × *nearly/*+ *almost be regarded as imminent*. She felt × *nearly/*+ *almost a prisoner*.)

ll. 5—6 trat er in die Armee ein: + *he entered the army;* + *he enrolled in the army.*
ll. 6—7 und nahm ... am Krieg teil: + *and served during the war;* (+) *and took part in the war;* (+) *and participated in the war* (latter 2 verbs more suitable with other activities, e.g. games, projects, sports).
l. 6 als Nachrichtenoffizier: + *as a communications officer;* + *as a radio officer;* + *as an officer in the Intelligence Service;* + *as an officer in Intelligence* (less formal); + *as an Intelligence officer.* (It is not clear from the ST which of these [very different] activities he was involved in).

> A further scholarship secured him a place in one of the less snobbish colleges, where he made the acquaintance of Philip Larkin and John Wain. The friendship which bound him to both [men] has left its traces in the works of all three writers.

l. 7 ... verschaffte ihm Einlaß: + *secured/gained his admission to/ into;* + *secured/gained his entrance to;* + *granted him access/ admission to;* (+) *gave him the possibility to attend...* (Simple Aspect required here.)
ll. 8—9 wo er P. L. und J. W. kennenlernte: non-defining relative clause; hence comma obligatory. + *where he became acquainted with P. L. and J. W.;* + *where he got to know P. L. and J. W.* (less formal).
ll. 9—10 ..., die ihn mit beiden verband: a defining relative clause; thus no commas! + *... uniting him with both;* + *... uniting/which united the three of them;* × *which was uniting...;* (+) *which he felt for both [of them];* × *which tied him to both* (suggests negative aspect. cf. "She's very tied to her parents".); × *which linked/connected/joined him to both.*
l. 10 hinterließ: tense: Simple Past or Present Perfect possible here.
l. 10 ... hinterließ ihre Spuren...: + *left its mark on;* (+) *left its stamp on;* + *can be traced in.* Or: + *The work of all three writers bore the mark of the friendship....*
ll. 10—11 aller drei Schriftsteller: (+) *of all the three writers/authors.*

> Just as the majority of the other college inmates they hailed from comparable social backgrounds and shared the same problems: bewilderment at the continuance of academic ineffectiveness, of scholarly lack of commitment and of self-conceit; bewilderment at [the] arrogant claim to authority, at naive belief in tradition, and at cultural philistinism.

ll. 11—12: Sie kamen ... aus ...: + *they came from;* + *they originated from;* (+) *they were from;* × *they came out of;* × *they stemmed from.*
l. 11 wie: + *as;* + *like.*
l. 11 der anderen College-Insassen: + *the other college fellows;* + *the other fellow students;* (+) *their peers/contemporaries* (= of same age; studying at the same time).
ll. 12—13 aus vergleichbaren sozialen Verhältnissen: + *from similar social backgrounds/circumstances;* × *conditions* (has broader reference than context here [family status] cf. "Social conditions in the 19th century were rather poor.").
ll. 13—17 die Verwirrung ... Kulturphilistertum: this section has particular difficulties: (a) interpretation of the meaning of the ST abstract nouns; (b) use of definite article; (c) syntax.
l. 13 die Verwirrung: (+) *the bewilderment/confusion at ...* (use of definite article possible, though unlikely, here as the abstract noun is particularised by following prepositional modification). + *confusion about ...;* (+) *bewilderment about.*
l. 14 die Fortdauer: + *the continuation of ...;* + *the continuing ...;* (+) *the duration of ... .*
l. 14 des akademischen Leerlaufs: (a) Note: zero article with abstract noun used without specific reference. (b) + *of academic ineffectuality;* + *of academic inefficacy;* (where "Leerlauf" is interpreted as "action but with little or no effect"). (+) *... idling;* (+) *... lack of activity* (in the latter two cases "Leerlauf" is interpreted much more negatively, suggesting laziness on the part of academics).
ll. 14—15 der gelehrsamen Unverbindlichkeit: (a) (+) *of [the] scholarly lack of commitment* (zero article more likely). (b) repeat "of" to make genitive reference clear in ET; (c) (+) *of [the] learned lack of commitment;* × *of scholarly irresponsibility* (too negative); (+) *of the scholarly, non-commital attitude.* Note: clash between "gelehrsam" (in this context = putting on airs of intellectuality) and "Unverbindlichkeit" (= lack of commitment).
l. 15 und Selbstbespiegelung: + *self-adulation;* + *self-centredness;* + *egotism;* (+) *self-admiration;* × *narcissism* (too physical); × *self-complacency* (= self-satisfaction); × *self-complacence* (= self-satisfaction); × *self-indulgence* (ambiguous: (a) = + holding an unrealistically positive view of oneself; (b) = × gratifying one's own inclinations and desires); × *self-observation;* × *introspection.*
ll. 15—16 über Autoritätsanmaßung ...: (a) to render backreference to

"die Verwirrung", indicated by ST "über", ET needs to repeat the noun: "bewilderment at"! (b) + *at presumptuous authority* (zero article!); (+) *at [the] pretence to authority;* × *at [the] usurpation of authority* (although postmodifying "of"-prepositional phrase makes use of definite article possible, zero article implies more general reference. "Usurpation" usually used in political context: of power, of a throne).
l. 16 Traditionsgläubigkeit: (a) repeat preposition "at" in ET to avoid ambiguity of reference. (b) + *at blind belief in tradition[s];* (+) *at the blind/naive belief in tradition[s]* (use of definite article possible [owing to prepositional postmodification of "belief"] but unlikely); + *at traditionalism;* × *at credulity in/of tradition[s].*
ll. 16—17 und Kulturphilistertum: (a) in "model" ET comma before "and" obligatory; (otherwise this prepositional phrase would post-modify "belief"!) (b) again repeat preposition "at" in ET to avoid ambiguity of reference. (c) (+) *..., and at cultural narrow-mindedness/pedantry/ lack of imagination.*

> According to his own words Amis felt at home at St. John's College; not only because he met kindred spirits there(,) but also because most of his fellow-students were intelligent and hard-working and did not wish to have anything to do with the cult of failure(,) which was to become fashionable a decade later.

l. 17 nach seinen Worten: (a) best placed initially in ET. (b) + *In his own words;* + *According to his own account;* + *Amis says/said himself that ... .*
l. 17 Amis fühlte sich wohl: + *Amis felt/was happy;* + *Amis felt at ease;* (+) *Amis enjoyed being* (might suggest frivolity); (+) *Amis liked to be;* (+) *felt comfortable;* × *felt well* (refers to state of physical health); × *felt good* (too informal here); × *was feeling happy ... .*
ll. 17—18 am St. John's College: × *in St. John's College* (= inside the building. It is the institution [and not merely the building] that is referred to here; thus "at" should be used).
l. 18 Gleichgesinnte: (+) *like-minded friends.*
l. 19 ..., weil die meisten seiner Kommilitonen ...: (a) no comma in ET after "but also". (b) + *the majority of ...;* ⊗ *the most of ... .*
l. 20 fleißig: + *sedulous;* + *assiduous;* + *persevering;* (+) *diligent* (but repetition of "-igent" [after "intelligent"] undesirable from a stylistic point of view); (+) *industrious* (mainly for practical or manual work); × *efficient* (= competent; skilled; producing a desired result).

ll. 20—21 und von dem ... nichts wissen wollten: + *did not want to be associated with;* × *and did not want to know anything about* (= did not desire information about...).
l. 20 von dem Kult des Versagens: + *with the glorification of failure.*
**ll. 20—21 ..., wie er eine Dekade später Mode wurde, ...:* (a) this relative clause can be interpreted as defining (without commas) but is more likely to be non-defining (with commas). (b) + *which became fashionable...;* + *which became/was to become the fashion/the trend...;* + *which came/was to come into fashion...* . (Note: use of "was to" typical for reference to future destiny from past point of view.) (c) If "wie" is translated by "as", beware! + *as became fashionable...;* × *as it became fashionable...* (= clause of reason).

> Although the main character of his first best-selling novel — Jim Dixon — also bears autobiographical traits, the attempt to equate Amis with Dixon or to recast the latter as a positive hero is just as questionable as the assertion sometimes made that Amis has nothing more that is remarkable to say.

l. 22 die Hauptgestalt: + *the main figure;* +*the principal character/figure.*
l. 22 Erfolgsromanes: + *successful novel.*
l. 23 autobiographische Züge trägt: + *shows autobiographical traits/features.*
l. 24 Amis mit Dixon gleichzusetzen: + *to identify A. with D.;* + *to see A. and D. as one and the same person;* × *to put A. on a par with D.* (= to put him on the same level as).
ll. 24—25 oder letzteren in einen positiven Helden umzumünzen: + *or to remodel/remould the latter as a positive hero;* + *or to reshape the latter as/into a positive hero;* + *or to transform/convert/change the latter into a positive hero;* × *or to recoin the latter...* (cf. to coin a phrase = to invent a new phrase or expression).
l. 25 ebenso ... wie: × *is equally ... as* (unidiomatic); ⊗ *is just so ... as* (negative clauses permit both "not as ... as" and "not so ... as". In assertive clauses, however, "as ... as" must be used).
l. 25 fragwürdig: (+) *doubtful;* (+) *suspect;* (+) *debatable;* (+) *disputable.*
ll. 25—26 wie die manchmal geäußerte Behauptung: + *as the assertion/statement [which is] sometimes made/uttered;* + *as the opinion [which is] sometimes voiced/expressed/expressed from time to time/from time*

to time expressed ⊗ as the opinion [which is] sometimes maintained; ⊗ as the sometimes expressed opinion. (Postmodification required here. See notes to A 1, l. 4; ll. 18—19; A 3, ll. 9—10; ll. 16—18.)

ll. 26—27 nichts weiter Bemerkenswertes: (a) Beware: relative clause required here to avoid mistranslation: × *nothing more remarkable* (ambiguous = "nichts Bemerkenswerteres" [uttered in one breath group]); or = "nichts weiter Bemerkenswertes" (if a pause occurs after "more"). Alternatively: + *nothing else remarkable.* (b) Bemerkenswertes: + *noteworthy;* + *worthy of note.*

l. 27 zu sagen: + *to relate;* + *to tell us;* × *to tell.*

> Speaking of Jim Dixon Amis comments that during his life hitherto Dixon has always seen how power and rank fell to those who distinguished themselves less by their abilities than by their smooth manners, their refined accent(,) and the influence [which] they or their fathers were able to bring to bear.

l. 27 Amis bemerkt über Jim Dixon: + *Speaking of/about Jim Dixon Amis remarks/notes that...;* + *Amis makes the remark about J. D. that....*

l. 27 dieser: + *that his hero/character;* × *he* (reference is ambiguous); (+) *the latter* (only acceptable if "Jim Dixon" has followed "Amis" in the preceding clause).

l. 28 während seines bisherigen Lebens: + *during his life up to that time;* × *during his life up to now.* (The time reference here is to the point of time at which Amis made this remark, and not to the moment when the statement is read.)

l. 28 habe ... gesehen: tense: present perfect (Not past perfect!) is required here since the indirect speech is introduced by a verb in the present tense. The subsequent verbs in this sentence ("zufielen", "hervortraten", "ausüben konnten") may be (consistently) rendered by either Simple Past or by Present Perfect tense.

l. 28 stets: position should be medial: + *Dixon has always seen.* × *always has seen* (only when auxiliary verb is stressed for contrastive focus).

l. 29 Macht: + *authority;* (+) *influence;* × *might;* × *strength;* × *force;* × *potency.*

l. 29 Stellung: + *position;* + *station.* (See "model" for the preferable ET collocation of the two nouns.)

l. 29 zufielen: + *accrued/* + *have accrued to ...;* + *were accrued by/* + *have been accrued by ....*
l. 29 denen ..., die: × *those ones who;* × *the ones who.* (Note: no comma after "those": defining relative clause!)
ll. 29—30 weniger durch ... als durch ...: + *not so much on account of ... as on account of ...* (Note word order: + *who distinguished themselves not so much ...);* + *not so much because of ... as because of ....*
l. 30 ihre glatten Manieren: + *their polished/easy manners.*
ll. 30—31 "gebildeten": + *"cultivated";* + *"educated";* + *"cultured";* + *"well-bred".*
ll. 31—32 ..., den sie ... ausüben konnten: (a) Defining relative clause (hence no commas!). Relative pronoun optional: *[which/that].* (b) + *... were able to/have been able to/could exert/wield;* (+) *... [to] exercise* (cf. to exercise power/authority). × *... [to] practise* (cf. to practise law, medicine, a profession, a sport); × *[to] carry on* (cf. to carry on a trade).

> This new type of hero is a somewhat "slovenly" young man(,) who is confused but not really impressed by a social hierarchy which passes itself off as the natural order of things or by a leading class which asserts [the] privileges it has claimed for itself.

l. 33 ein etwas "vergammelter" junger Mann: (a) + *a rather "slovenly" young man;* (b) "vergammelter" refers primarily to outward appearance but can also refer to mental attitude. Thus: + *"slovenly";* + *"hippie-like";* + *"beatnik-like"* (the two latter retaining the ST reference to "Gammler" and the colloquial idiom); (+) *"dishevelled";* (+) *"unkempt"* (the two latter refer solely to outward appearance); (+) *"seedy"* (more informal; tends to refer to outward appearance only); (+) *"degenerate"* (possibly too negative; may refer to both outward appearance and mental attitude). (c) × *... youth* (= [approx.] a teenager; thus possibly too young here).
ll. 33—34 ..., der verwirrt ...: comma in ET optional here as the relative clause can be understood as either defining or non-defining. The former interpretation is, however, more likely in this context (= without comma).
ll. 34—35 von einer Gesellschaftshierarchie, die ...: No comma in ET (defining relative clause). See also l. 36: "Schicht, die ...", where the same applies.

ll. 35—36 . . ., die sich als selbstverständlich ausgibt: + . . . *which poses as/presents itself as the natural order of things;* + *which declares itself to be the natural order of things;* + *which feigns to be the natural order of things;* (+) *which poses as/presents itself as natural;* × *which . . . as a foregone conclusion/as a matter of course/as self-evident.*
ll. 36—37 . . ., die angemaßte Vorrechte geltend macht: + . . . *which/that exercises/pretends to/asserts [the] privileges/prerogatives it has claimed for itself/presumed/usurped;* (+) . . . *which/that exercises/pretends to/asserts/claims usurped privileges* ("usurped" rather too strong here. It is usually power, authority, position, a throne, a crown that is usurped).

> A totally negative verdict is pronounced in 1955 by Somerset Maugham, [who was] then over 80 years old. Despite the fact that he, among others, is convinced of Amis' talent as a writer he [nevertheless] regards the latter's characters as scum. In his view they do not go to university to gain culture but [rather] to obtain a post; as soon as they have one they go to rack and ruin. He goes on to say that they have no manners and are incapable of coping with difficulties in the social sphere. Maugham expresses his satisfaction that he will no longer be living by the time this generation is represented in Parliament.

l. 38 Ein völlig ablehnendes Urteil fällt . . . Somerset Maugham: + *A totally negative/damning verdict/judgement is/was passed/pronounced by S. M.;* + *He receives/received an absolute rebuff from S. M.;* + *He is/was totally rejected by S. M.* For a more neutral, less harsh interpretation: + *A totally negative opinion is/was given by S. M.* (Note: either Simple Present [as in ST] or Simple Past acceptable here.)
ll. 38—39 der damals über 80jährige Somerset Maugham: (a) Postmodification (see "model" translation) is preferable — a non-defining relative (or reduced) relative clause; hence comma compulsory. (b) Premodification is nevertheless just about possible here, albeit rather heavy: (+) *by the then over 80-year-old S. M.* (Note: if the time adverbial is expanded into a phrase ["at that time"], this premodifying construction would be rendered too weighty to be feasible.) (c) Note that in the premodifying attributive phrase the singular of "year" (with hyphens) is used: + *by the then over 80-year-old S. M.* ⊗ *by the then over 80-years-old S. M.* cf. + *by S. M., [who was] then over 80 years old.*

ll. 38—39: word order: (a) (+) *A totally negative verdict was pronounced by Somerset Maugham, then over 80 years old, in 1955.* (Although this sentence may be correct grammatically, it is unacceptable as too much focus is lent to the time adverbial "in 1955", thus altering the information focus of the sentence (see UGE, chap. 14). (b) If an active construction is used, it is still better to reserve, as in ST, the completely new information (Somerset Maugham etc.) for the end of the sentence, where it receives the greatest focus (see UGE, chap. 14), and where it provides a logical link to the subsequent sentence. Thus: + *He received an absolute rebuff in 1955 from ... S. M.;* × *S. M. ... gave him an absolute rebuff in 1955.*

ll. 39—41: Zwar ... jedoch ...: + *It is true that he ... but/yet he ...;* + *Although he ...(,) he ....*

l. 39 auch er: × *he is also convinced ...* (Use of "also" not strictly logical as no others have been mentioned.) × *even he ...* (wrong meaning).

ll. 39—40 von Amis' schriftstellerischem Talent: + *of Amis'/Amis's literary talent;* × *... literal ...* (= word for word; following the actual words of a text without interpretation).

l. 40 dessen: greater clarity is achieved by using + *the latter's;* (+) *his.*

ll. 40—41 hält ... für Abschaum: (a) + *regards/considers ... as/to be scum.* (b) + *dross* (lit. = scum of melting metals; fig. = s.th. worthless; (+) *dregs* (lit. = sediment e.g. of wine (thus image different from ST; fig. = s.th. worthless); × *refuse.*

ll. 41—48: (a) This section contains indirect thought, expressed in ST by the subjunctive. To render this unambiguously in ET make use of such phrases as "in his view/opinion"; "he thought"/"thinks"; "he claimed"/"claims" etc. (See "model" translation.) (b) Tenses: in this section consistent use of either Simple Present or Simple Past is permissible, if a non-verbal indicator of indirect thought (e.g. "in his view"/"in his opinion") is used. With the indirect thought introduced by a verb, the tense used to express the indirect thought will depend on the tense used for the introductory verb: thus: + *He thinks they do not go to university .../+ He thought they did not go to university ....*

l. 41 ... gingen nicht auf die Universität: + *... not go to university/ go up to university/attend university;* + *... go to the university*

(+ AmE. In BE = go to the building, e.g. as student or tourist, rather than to the institution, as a student).
I. 42 um sich Kultur anzueignen: + *[in order] to acquire/absorb culture.*
II. 42—43 um eine Stellung zu bekommen: + *to obtain a position;* (+) *to get a job* (rather informal).
I. 43 hätten sie erst eine: + *once they had one;* × *first they had one;* × *not until they had one.*
I. 43 würden sie darin verlottern: (a) + *they would go to rack and ruin.* (Note use of "would" to express habitual action possible here.) (b) + *they squandered/would squander their talents* (more formal than subsequent alternatives [ST informal]); + *they went/would go to seed;* + *they went/would go to the dogs.*
I. 44 und seien unfähig...: + *and were not capable of -ing...;* ⊗ *and were incapable to/not capable to....*
II. 44—45 mit Schwierigkeiten... fertig zu werden: + *... of coming to terms/grips with difficulties...;* + *... of dealing satisfactorily/successfully with difficulties...;* (+) *... of tackling difficulties* (= confronting them).
I. 45 Bereich: × *field* (cf. technical field; scientific field; field of vision; field of duty); × *area;* × *region;* × *zone;* × *province;* × *domain;* × *realm* (mainly geographical or political); × *range;* × *scope.*
I. 46 nicht mehr zu leben: + *he will no longer be alive;* × *he will no longer live;* × *not to live any more.*
I. 47 wenn... erst einmal: = (approx.) *when this point of time has arrived* ("erst einmal" intensifies "wenn"). × *if...* (reference here is clearly temporal). + *once this generation...;* (+) *when this generation is finally...;* × *when this generation is... for the first time.*
II. 47—48 vertreten sein werde: The tense required here is Simple Present! ⊗ *... by the time/once this generation will be represented.* (Remember: no future tense in subordinate clauses of time.)

Text 2: Wissenschaftliche Prüfung für das Lehramt an den Gymnasien, 1976/I

England ist eine Insel. Man lernt dies in der Schule und glaubt es dann zu wissen; aber erst wenn man hinreist, erfährt man es. Man ist gezwungen, die Erde zu verlassen, das trotz all seiner Erfindungen dem Mensch gemäße Element, und sich der Luft oder dem Wasser anzuvertrauen. Noch vor dreißig Jahren erregten die Kanalschiffe die Phantasie der Knaben und Defraudanten. Auf kleinen deutschen Bahnhöfen hingen unter den Fahrplänen des Lokalverkehrs weißblaue Plakate, die einen bärtigen Seemann in Sturmkleidung zeigten, der mit starken Armen Hoek van Holland und Harwich umspannte, und zwischen seinen mächtigen Händen plätscherte das weite Meer und schwamm der zuverlässige Dampfer der Gesellschaft vom Kontinent zur Insel.
Die Plakate sind verschwunden, Knaben und Kassierer träumen von dem Flugzeug, das über den Atlantik oder über den Pol fliegt, aber das Kanalschiff sieht heute noch genau wie auf den alten Bildern aus, sauber und zuverlässig, so liegt es in Hoek am Kai. Leuchtfeuer, Nebelhörner, Möwengekreisch und der Salzgeschmack der Luft vermitteln dem Binnenländer das Abenteuer Seefahrt, dem er für ein paar Stunden sich hingeben will ...
In Harwich teilt man die Menschheit in Briten und in Fremde. Der Engländer, der noch am Abend nichts als ein Mitreisender war, ist am Morgen als Brite erwacht. Stolz erhobenen Hauptes schreitet er an den Fremden vorbei zu einer nur für ihn weit geöffneten Pforte; es ist eine Heimkehr des verlorenen Sohnes, und die anderen Reisenden warten wie Bittsteller vor einer verschlossenen, von Polizisten bewachten Tür. Am liebsten, so scheint es, ließe man den Fremden nicht ein in das gelobte Land, und man versucht mit Bürokratie der bedauerlichen Lage, einige dieser undurchschaubaren Subjekte doch hereinlassen zu müssen, Herr zu werden. Draußen vor der englischen Tür versteht man nicht, daß Casanova und Karl Marx und Revolutionäre und Königsmörder ohne Zahl nach England als nach der Insel der Freiheit flohen. Erst wenn man hinter der Tür, erst wenn man in England ist, begreift man

dies wieder. Der Polizist, ein weiblicher, wies mich zu einem Immigration-Officer, der wie ein Lehrer auf dem Katheder thronte, aber wie alle englischen Amtspersonen von an-
40 genehmstem Wesen, leise und überaus höflich war. Leider schien er mich für einen Propheten zu halten. Er wollte wissen, was ich in London tun, wo ich in London wohnen, wen ich in London sehen und wie lange ich in London bleiben würde. Wer kann das vorhersagen? Um den freundlichen Gentle-
45 man zu beruhigen, nannte ich ihm ein Hotel, das eine Erinnerung an Virginia Woolf war, doch hätte ich ihm ebensogut sagen können, daß ich bei Sherlock Holmes in Baker Street logieren wolle.

Aus: Bernhard Koeppen, Zauberwelt der roten Autobusse.

"Model" translation(s) and annotations (in sections)

Britain is an island. One learns this at school and thinks one has taken it in; but not until one travels there does one really comprehend what it means. One is obliged to leave the dry land, the element which in spite of all man's inventions is most suited to him, and [to] commit oneself to the air or the water.

I. 1 England ist eine Insel: "England" is clearly used imprecisely (as often in German) to denote Britain. What is meant here is the main island of Great Britain (including Scotland and Wales, but excluding its fourth constituent region: Northern Ireland). Thus: × *England is an island* is obviously untrue.
II. 1—2 Man: + *You* (more informal).
I. 1 in der Schule: + *in school* (AmE); × *in the school* (= in the building specifically).
II. 1—2 Man lernt dies in der Schule und glaubt es dann zu wissen: + *This is what/a fact one learns at school and subsequently thinks one knows;* + *One learns this at school and believes one knows [it]* (Although "it" is usually omitted after "to know" e.g. Ich weiß es = I know, it is optional here (reference to a specific fact); + *One is taught this at school and thinks one has registered it.*
II. 2—3 aber erst wenn man hinreist, erfährt man es: + *but not before/ only when one goes there does one really comprehend what it means;*

⊗ *but not until/not before/only when one goes there one comprehends what it means.* (Inversion necessary following negative or restrictive word/phrase placed initially for emphasis.) Alternatively a cleft sentence could be used: + *but it is not until/not before/only when one goes there that one comprehends what it means.*
II. 2—3 erfahren + es: + *come to know [it];* + *find [it] out;* + *experience it;* (+) *discover it.*
l. 3 Man ist gezwungen: + *One is compelled to ...;* (+) *One is forced to ...* (These alternatives are progressively stronger than "model" ET.)
l. 3 die Erde zu verlassen: + *to leave/abandon dry land;* + *to leave land;* × *to leave the land* (suggests move from country to town); × *to leave the ground* (suggests flight only); ⊗ *to leave ground;* × *to leave the earth* (suggests space flight).
II. 3—4 das trotz all seiner Erfindungen dem Mensch gemäße Element: + *..., the element which despite all man's inventions is appropriate to/ for him, ...*
l. 5 sich ... anzuvertrauen: + *to entrust oneself to;* + *to give oneself up to;* (+) *to take to;* × *to put oneself in the hands of.*
l. 5 der Luft oder dem Wasser: + *to the air or the sea;* + *to air or water;* + *to air or sea.* (Style: keep use of definite article parallel here.)

> Only thirty years ago the cross-channel ferries [still] stirred the imagination[s] of lads and frauds. At small railway stations in Germany, hung below the timetables for local services, were posters in blue and white depicting a bearded seaman in oilskins embracing with [his] sturdy arms the Hook of Holland and Harwich. And between his mighty hands splashed the wide open sea(,) across which the reliable company steamer made its way from the continent to the island.

l. 6 Kanalschiffe: + *channel boats;* × *channel ships.*
l. 6 erregten ... die Phantasie: + *excited/aroused the imagination[s];* × *fantasy* (esp. in psychological terminology); (+) *inspired ...;* × *agitated ...;* × *stimulated ....* Simple Past obligatory ("Thirty years ago").
II. 6—7 der Knaben und Defraudanten: (a) zero article (general, non-specific reference); (b) + *of youths/boys and swindlers/cheats.*
II. 7—9 Auf kleinen deutschen Bahnhöfen ... in Sturmkleidung zeigten: + *At small German railway stations, below the timetables for local*

services, hung blue and white posters which depicted a seaman in oilskins . . . . Note: (a) style: take care that the defining relative clause (or reduced relative clause as in "model" translation) follows directly after the noun to which it refers ("posters"). This is made possible by inversion of main verb and its subject (common when place adjunct is positioned initially and an existential verb (or substitute) is used. (See UGE, Chap. 14.) (b) × *blue and white posters hung which* . . . (unacceptable since i) style: relative clause should preferably follow directly after noun it refers to; ii) final position in clause for the verb "hung" gives the latter too great emphasis.

l. 8 unter den Fahrplänen des Lokalverkehrs: + *below/beneath/under the timetables for local lines;* + *below the local timetables;* (+) *below the timetables for local transport* (= all means).

ll. 8—9 weißblaue Plakate: (+) *white and blue* (unidiomatic: "blue and white", like "fish and chips", "knives and forks", invariably appears in this order).

l. 9 zeigten: + *displaying;* + *showing;* + . . . *with/of a bearded seaman* . . . .

ll. 10—11 der mit starken Armen Hoek van Holland und Harwich umspannte: word order: (+) *embracing the Hook of Holland and Harwich with his strong arms* (this ET inferior as end-focus naturally falls on the place names here. Also, following the principle of endweight, the longer item tends to take up final position (see UGE, chap. 14).

ll. 11—13 und zwischen seinen . . . Händen . . . zur Insel: word order in "model" translation: see notes to II. 7—9. Also: + *and between his mighty hands the wide open sea splashed and the reliable company steamer made its way from the continent to the island.* (This ET gives greater emphasis to "splashed".)

l. 11 plätscherte: (+) *rippled* (with slight gentle waves, possibly accompanied by light, soft sound); × *gurgled;* × *babbled* (both used to refer to gentle flow of water over stones in streams or brooks).

l. 12 schwamm: + *sailed;* (use simple Aspect); × *swam* (only persons, fish, animals); × *floated* (= without sinking, but involving no movement in a particular direction); × *drifted* (= moved at the mercy of the wind, current or tide; thus incompatible with the context here of "der zuverlässige Dampfer").

> The posters have disappeared; lads and cashiers dream of the aeroplane on its Atlantic or transpolar flight but [even] today the cross-channel ferry still looks exactly as it did in the old pictures, clean and reliable — that is how it lies at the quay in the Hook. Beacons, fog horns, the cries of seagulls and the salty tang of the air convey to the inlander the feeling of a seafaring adventure(,) which he willingly indulges in for a few hours.

l. 14 sind verschwunden: + *have vanished.* Present Perfect required here.

ll. 14—15 träumen von: + *are dreaming of/about.* (Simple Aspect more likely.)

l. 15 Flugzeug: + *airplane* (AmE).

ll. 15—16 das über den Atlantik oder über den Pol fliegt: Note how the "model" ET avoids the rather unusual use of "Pole" alone in English, i.e. without specifying whether the North or the South Pole. Alternatively: (+) *which/that flies over/across the Atlantic or over the Pole.* (Style: to enable use of 2 parallel phrases preferably use "over".)

ll. 16—17 aber das Kanalschiff sieht heute noch genau wie auf den alten Bildern aus: (a) word order: ⊗ *but today the cross-channel ferry looks still exactly as...;* ⊗ *...looks still today exactly as....* (b) + *...looks just as it did...;* × *...looks exactly/just like it did...* (Although such phrases as the latter are commonly heard in spoken English, they are strictly speaking incorrect grammatically. "As" should be used when a verb follows in the clause or is implied.)

ll. 16—17 auf den alten Bildern: + *in/on the old photos/photographs;* × *on the old pictures.*

ll. 17—18 ..., sauber und zuverlässig, so liegt es in Hoek am Kai: + *...clean and reliable, moored at the quay in/at the Hook;* +..., *clean and reliable — thus it lies at the quay in/at the Hook.*

l. 17 zuverlässig: + *dependable;* × *trustworthy* (mainly for persons).

l. 18 Möwengekreisch: + *the shrieks of seagulls* (loud, [usually unpleasant], shrill cry); (+) *the screeching/screeches of seagulls* (loud, unpleasant, grating sound). Note: "model" ET uses usual or neutral word for "Möwengekreisch".

l. 19 der Salzgeschmack: + *the salty taste;* + *the salt tang/taste.*

l. 19 vermitteln: + *impart to;* + *give.*

l. 19 dem Binnenländer: (+) *the landlubber* (= person not accustomed to leaving dry land. Does not refer to place or residence); × *the* *continental* (= seen from the British point of view, a European [excluding the British]. But includes both inlanders and coastal dwellers); × *the mainlander* (also includes both inlanders and coastal dwellers).

ll. 19—20 ... das Abenteuer Seefahrt, dem er ...: The main problem here is to get the correct reference of the relative clause in ET (i.e. referring to "adventure" and not to "voyage"): + ... *the [feeling of the] adventure of a sea voyage — an adventure he ...;* × ... *the [feeling of the] adventure of a sea voyage(,) which he ....*

ll. 20—21 ..., dem er ... sich hingeben will: + ..., *which he willingly submits himself to/gives himself up to.*

> At Harwich mankind is divided into British subjects and aliens. The Englishman(,) who only the evening before was a mere fellow-traveller(,) has awoken in the morning as a British subject. [With] his head proudly held high he strides past the aliens to a gate [which is] opened wide only for him; it is a return of the prodigal son and the other travellers wait like petitioners at a locked door which is guarded by policemen.

l. 22 In Harwich: + *In Harwich.*
l. 22 die Menschheit: (+) *the human race;* (+) *humanity;* × *man.*
l. 22 teilt man: (+) *they divide* (more informal; stylistically inferior to use of passive as in "model"); × *one divides;* × *people divide.*
l. 22 in Briten und Fremde: The two signs one actually sees at the customs checkpoints on arrival in Britain are "British subjects" and "Aliens". (+) *Britons/Britishers and foreigners;* × *strangers.*
l. 23 Der Engländer, der ...: in ET comma optional (relative clause may be interpreted as either defining or non-defining).
l. 23 noch am Abend: + *the previous evening;* × *still in the evening.*
l. 23 nichts als: + *no more than;* (+) *nothing but.*
l. 24 ist am Morgen als Brite erwacht: (a) Present Perfect or Simple Present required: + *awakes;* (b) + *has woken up/wakes up* (more informal); (c) + *as a British subject* (indefinite article obligatory); (d) word order: (+) *has awoken as a British subject in the morning* (gives unnaturally strong emphasis to the time adjunct, which should therefore be placed earlier [See UGE chap. 14]).
ll. 24—25 stolz erhobenen Hauptes: + *[With] his head proudly raised;* + *With [his] head proudly raised aloft;* (+) *With his nose in the air* (informal; possibly too negative here); + *With his head held high he*

proudly strides... (Although "stolz", in fact, modifies "erhobenen Haupes" this translation is acceptable as in this context the meaning is barely changed.)

l. 25 schreitet er: (a) + *he stalks* (= proudly and with long steps); + *he marches* (in military fashion); (+) *he struts* (= proudly but as a peacock or a fashion mannequin, showing off); × *he paces* (= i) with measured steps (e.g. to pace out a room); ii) walks nervously up and down (e.g. in anticipation of important news); (b) Use simple Aspect.

ll. 25—26 zu einer nur für ihn weit geöffneten Pforte: post-modification required in ET here (see notes to A 1, l. 4; ll. 18—19; A 3, ll. 9—10, ll. 16—18: ⊗ *to a for him wide opened gate;* + *to a gate opened wide only to admit him/only for his admission*). In reality the "Pforte" resembles a gate rather than a door.

l. 27 warten: Avoid Progressive Aspect. Here it is a question of a habitual situation.

ll. 27—28 wie Bittsteller: + *like supplicants;* × *as petitioners/ supplicants.* (They only resemble petitioners; they are not here in this capacity. cf. "She spoke like a teacher" [= in the manner of...]; "she spoke as a teacher" [= in the capacity of...].)

l. 28 vor einer verschlossenen, von Polizisten bewachten Tür: a combination of premodification and post-modification is required here. See "model" ET; see note to A 1, l. 4 ll. 18—19; A 3, ll. 9—10; ll. 16—18: (a) + *at/before/in front of a closed/locked gate that/which is [being] guarded by policemen/[the] police;* (Note: avoid using a reduced relative clause here: × *wait like petitioners at a locked gate guarded by policemen* as it would be unclear whether it is the petitioners or the gate that is being guarded.); × *at a locked police-guarded gate* (too weighty); (b) "Tür": may be translated as "door" here to offer alternative translation (ST: "Pforte" l. 26; "Tür" l. 28). Otherwise repeat "gate" (see note to ll. 25—26).

> They would, it seems, prefer not to admit the alien into the promised land and with bureaucracy they try to cope with the lamentable situation of nevertheless being obliged to admit some of these suspicious elements. Outside the gateway into Britain people cannot understand that Casanova and Karl Marx and countless numbers of revolutionaries and regicides fled to Britain as the isle of liberty. Not until one passes through the gate, not until one is inside Britain(,) can one comprehend this again.

l. 29 Am liebsten ... ließe man den Fremden nicht ein: + *They would prefer not to allow the alien to enter the promised land;* + *They would prefer not to allow the alien into the promised land;* + *They would rather/sooner* (more informal) *refuse the alien admission to the promised land.*
l. 30 das gelobte Land: + *the promised land* (as in bible); × *the land of promise* (modern expression = with good prospects).
l. 30 mit Bürokratie: + *with bureaucratic means/rules;* + *with red tape* (more informal). Preferably placed initially in clause owing to presence of multiple object. Alternatively make use of an insertion: + *and they try, with bureaucracy, to ... .*
ll. 30—32 ... der bedauerlichen Lage Herr zu werden: + *to master/to overcome the unfortunate/regrettable/deplorable situation/state of affairs ... .*
l. 32 ... doch hereinlassen zu müssen: + *... of nevertheless having to admit ...;* + *... of having nevertheless to admit;* (+) *of still having to admit ...* (ambiguous: "still" could be interpreted temporally); ⊗ *... of having still to admit ...*
l. 31 einige dieser undurchschaubaren Subjekte: + *some of these suspicious/obscure characters/types/fellow mortals/fellow creatures* (all fairly colloquial as in ST).
ll. 32—33 Draußen vor der englischen Tür: + *Outside the gateway/gate/door into/to Britain/England;* × *In front of ...* (not clear which side of the entrance). × *Behind ... .*
l. 34 Revolutionäre und Königsmörder ohne Zahl: + *countless numbers of/innumerable/numberless revolutionaries and regicides/murderers of kings/assassins of kings;* (+) *kings' murderers.* (Note: regicide = the crime or the person committing such a crime.)
l. 35 der Insel der Freiheit: + *the island of liberty;* (+) *the isle/island of freedom.* (In general political sense "Freiheit", if unqualified, is usually translated by "liberty".)
l. 35 flohen: Both Simple Past and Present Perfect tenses are possible here, depending on whether one sees the time span implied as having concluded at some point in the past or whether one sees the time span as continuing up to the present. With the mention of Casanova and Karl Marx the former is more likely.
ll. 35—36 Erst wenn man hinter der Tür (ist): + *Only when/Not before one is through the gate/has passed through the gate/is inside the gate;* × *behind the gate.*

l. 36 in England: + *inside Britain/England;* + *in Britain.*
ll. 36—37 begreift man dies wieder: (a) inversion required (see notes to ll. 2—3). Alternatively use cleft sentence: + *It is not until/only when one passes through the gate ... that one understands this again.*
(b) Use: + *to understand/* + *to come to understand/* + *to realize.*

> The police officer, a female, directed me to an immigration officer(,) who sat majestically like a schoolmaster at a high desk but who, like all English officials, was of the most pleasant manner, soft-voiced and extremely courteous. Unfortunately he appeared to take me for a prophet. He wanted to know what I was going to do in London, where I was going to stay in London, who[m] I was going to see in London and how long I was going to remain in London. Who can predict such things? To reassure the amiable gentleman I named a hotel [that] I recalled from Virginia Woolf but I could just as well have told him that I wanted to take rooms with Sherlock Holmes in Baker Street.

l. 37 Der Polizist, ein weiblicher: + *The police constable, a woman;* (+) *The policewoman;* × *the policeman, a woman.*
l. 37 wies mich zu...: + *ushered me to...;* + *sent me to...;* + *referred me to...;* + *showed me to...;* + *pointed out to me....*
ll. 38—39 ..., der wie ein Lehrer ... thronte: (a) This is most likely to be a non-defining relative clause, i.e. with comma. (Sitting at a high desk is unlikely to be a defining characteristic as this is how immigration officers usually present themselves to the public at a customs checkpoint.) (b) +*..., who was sitting/was seated majestically like a teacher;* +*..., who was enthroned like a schoolteacher;* +*..., who presided like a teacher;* × *..., who reigned...;* ⊗ *..., who throned....*
ll. 39—40 von angenehmstem Wesen, leise und überaus höflich war: (a) + *had the most pleasant manner, soft-voiced and extremely courteous;* + *had the most pleasant demeanour...;* (+) *was of the most pleasant nature/disposition...;* × *was of/had the most pleasant manners* (e.g. table manners. Refers to conventional etiquette); × *had the most pleasant character* (The interview would be too short to pass such judgement); × *had the most pleasant constitution* (= state of health); (b) **leise:** + *quiet;* + *calm;* (+) *gentle;* × *genteel;* (c) **überaus höflich:** + *exceedingly polite/courteous.*
ll. 42—44: ... was ich ... tun ... würde: + *what I would do...* + *what*

i intended/planned to do. (Whichever form you choose keep to it throughout the sentence.)

l. 44 Wer kann das vorhersagen?: + *Who can foretell this?;* (+) *Who can foretell/predict that?*

l. 41 freundlichen: +*amicable;* (+) *friendly;* × *kind.*

ll. 44—45 Um ... zu beruhigen: + *[In order] to set ... 's mind at rest;* + *To put ... at ease;* + *to please ...;* (+) *to keep ... happy* (informal); × *to appease* (= soothe the anger of); × *to pacify;* × *to calm;* × *to soothe;* × *to comfort*; × *to placate.*

l. 45 nannte ich ihm ein Hotel: (a) + *I gave him the name of a hotel;* × *I named him a hotel.* (b) + *an hotel.*

ll. 45—46 das eine Erinnerung an V. W. war: + *[which/that] I remembered from V. W.;* × *which reminded me of V. W.;* × *commemorating V. W.* (= in memory of her).

ll. 46—47 doch hätte ich ihm ebensogut sagen können: + *but I might just as well have said [to him];* ⊗ *but I might have told him just as well.*

ll. 47—48 daß ich bei Sherlock Holmes in Baker Street logieren wolle: + *[that] I wanted to take lodgings/lodge/stay with S. H. in Baker Street;* + *... at S. H.'s in Baker Street;* × *... by S. H. ... .*

Text 3: Wissenschaftliche Prüfung für das Lehramt an den Gymnasien, 1977/II

In seiner Auseinandersetzung mit Toynbee und dessen Interpretation der Weltgeschichte hat Ortega y Gasset gesagt, ein Engländer sei ein Mann, der sich damit befaßt, sich und andere darüber zu informieren, was in den verschiedenen Ländern vorgeht. Der spanische Weltbetrachter hielt seine Vorlesungen über Toynbees System, als König Georg VI. noch lebte, und so durfte er gerade noch jenes anscheinend selbstvergessene Interesse der Briten an den entlegensten Landschaften und Völkerstämmen voraussetzen, von dem er meinte, daß es auf ihrer 'Überlegenheit' beruht haben müsse. Der in vielen großartigen Unternehmungen gewonnene, über zwei Jahrhunderte haltbar gebliebene Erfolg, gekrönt durch tatsächlich ausgeübte Vorherrschaft, habe die Selbstsicherheit und auch die Muße verschafft, die es ihnen erlaubten, sich überall auf dem Erdball umzutun und die innere Ordnung des Inselreiches für garantiert zu erachten.
Ortega ging mit gewohntem Scharfsinn der Frage auf den Grund, wie es jenes rätselhafte Volk dahin gebracht habe, daß der Engländer als 'praktischer Mensch' schlechthin gelten konnte, obgleich es sich den Luxus leistete, jedes Jahr eine auserlesene Schar begabter junger Männer — wie Ortega sich ausdrückt — nach Oxford zu sperren, damit sie sich dort "außerhalb der Zeit" und ohne jeden Bezug zu praktischen Dingen mit Griechisch, Geschichte und Sport beschäftigen sollten. Der Spanier war nahe daran, diese als herrenmäßig aufgefaßte Verachtung eines atemlosen Zweckstudiums für eine der Ursachen der Überlegenheit zu halten und aus ihr jene eigentümliche Souveränität abzuleiten, die Briten auszuzeichnen pflegt, wenn sie später im Leben handelnd auftreten. Kurz, ihn erinnerte Oxford an das perikleische Zeitalter mit seiner schöpferischen Freiheit.
Heute stellt sich das alles in mancher Hinsicht anders dar. Der augenfälligste Unterschied aber scheint darin zu liegen, daß die Engländer sehr intensiv 'mit sich selbst' beschäftigt sind, während die übrige Welt, die einst ihr Blick umfaßte, auf eine durchaus normale Distanz zurückweicht. Inso-

weit bereits Ortega erste Anzeichen einer solchen insularen Entfremdung gewahrte, suchte er eine Erklärung in den durch Verkehr, Technik und Revolution bewirkten Veränderungen. Er
40 meinte, die seit dem Ende des Ersten Weltkrieges zu beobachtende Schrumpfung unseres Planeten habe das Inselreich allmählich seiner einzigartigen Sonderstellung beraubt. Und wirklich läßt sich mit guten Gründen behaupten, Großbritannien habe den archimedischen Punkt verloren, aus dem es
45 früher sein System der Herrschaft in Bewegung und im Gleichgewicht zu halten vermochte.

Hermann Proebst, Ein Kabinett aus Oxford.

"Model" translation(s) and annotations (in sections)

> In [the course of] his discussion of Toynbee and the latter's interpretation of world history(,) Ortega y Gasset remarked that an Englishman was someone [who was] concerned with informing himself and others about what was going on in the various countries.

I. 1 In seiner Auseinandersetzung mit Toynbee ... hat O. gesagt: + *Discussing Toynbee ... O. remarked;* + *O., in his discussion of Toynbee, remarked;* × *In his discussion with Toynbee...* (from the context it is clear that this is not a face-to-face interview between Toynbee and Ortega y Gasset). For "Auseinandersetzung" the ET requires an item compatible with an animate and inanimate ("Toynbee und dessen Interpretation..."): + *discourse on* (in this case avoid commencing with "In the course of"); × *controversy;* × *dispute;* × *argument;* × *altercation;* × *quarrel.*
I. 1 dessen: × *his* (reference ambiguous).
I. 2 der Weltgeschichte: (+) *of the history of the world* (very wordy); (+) *of the world's history* (unidiomatic); × *of the world history* (without a genitive modifier present (as in previous two examples) definite article not possible with subject names (cf. economics, world economics, the economics of world trade; politics, Western politics, the politics of the West).
I. 2 hat gesagt: (a) tense either Present Perfect (= expressed on some unspecified occasion before the present moment of speaking and still

readable today) or Simple Past (expressed on some occasion in past, unlinked to present moment). (b) + *[has] said;* + *[has] claimed.*

II. 2—5 ein Engländer sei ein Mann ... vorgeht: tenses in indirect speech: + *O. has said an Englishman is a man who is concerned... about what is going on....* (If Present Perfect is used to introduce indirect speech, present tense must be retained for the indirect speech. + *O. said an Englishman is/was a man who is/was concerned... about what is/was going on...* (If Simple Past introduces the indirect speech the tenses for the latter are normally moved one step further back into the past than the original wording of direct speech e.g. Simple Present → Simple Past. In this context, however, Present tense can be retained in indirect speech as the statement can be regarded as still holding true today. Whichever tense is chosen must be used consistently for the 3 verbs of indirect speech here.)

II. 2—3 ein Engländer sei ein Mann: + *an Englishman is/was a person...;* × *an Englishman was a man...* (this is not being disputed here! Besides, the repetition of "man" is rather ugly).

I. 3 der sich damit befaßt: + *who engages/[ed] in informing...;* + *who occupies/[ed] himself [with] informing...;* + *busies/[ed] himself [with] informing...;* + *whose concern [it] was to inform....*

II. 4—5 in den verschiedenen Ländern: × *in various countries* (= a selected few only); × *in the different countries* (= only those which differ.)

II. 4—5 ... was ... vorgeht: + *...about what is/was happening in...;* + *...about developments in...;* + *...about happenings in...;* × *...about the goings-on in...* (too colloquial here; also suggests trivial or scandalous activities.)

> The Spanish observer of world affairs gave his lectures on Toynbee's system when King George VI. was still alive and thus he was still just able to presuppose that apparently altruistic interest of the British in the most remote regions and races — an interest which in his view must have had its basis in their "superiority".

I. 5 Weltbetrachter: + *spectator mundi;* + *world observer;* (+) *spectator of world affairs;* (+) *contemplator of world affairs.*

II. 5—6 hielt seine Vorlesungen über: + *lectured on/about;* + *delivered his lectures on/about;* × *held his lectures.* Use Simple Past (not Progressive Aspect).

l. 6 noch lebte: + *was still living;* × *still lived.*
l. 7 und so: + *and therefore;* + *and so* (less formal).
ll. 7—8 jenes anscheinend selbstvergessene Interesse: + *that seemingly altruistic/unselfish/self-denying/self-oblivious interest;* ⊗ *self-forgotten.*
l. 8 den entlegensten Landschaften: (a) × *the furthest/farthest* (does not collocate with "races"); (b) + *lands* (rather literary); (+) *landscapes* (esp. of rural beauty; also works of art); × *scenery* (cf. "How the scenery changes as you drive south"); × *countryside* (cf. "We saw some beautiful countryside [scenery] on our trip").
l. 9 Völkerstämmen: + *peoples;* (+) *tribes* (restriction to primitive peoples).
l. 9 von dem . . . : care is needed here with the reference of the relative clause in ET: × *. . . in the most remote regions and races, which in his view must . . .* (Reference is ambiguous here, therefore unacceptable.) In such cases it is often useful to use a dash and, before introducing the relative clause, repeat the noun to which it refers (see "model" ET).
l. 9 er meinte: + *. . . which, he thought/believed, must . . .;* + *. . . which, in his opinion, must . . .*
l. 10 "Überlegenheit": + *ascendancy;* + *dominance;* + *dominant position.*

> The Spaniard claimed that their success, gained in many grand enterprises, prevailing for more than two centuries and crowned by predominance that was actually exercised, had secured them both the self-assurance and the leisure which enabled them to be active all over the globe and to consider the domestic order of the island realm [as] guaranteed.

ll. 10—12 Der . . . Erfolg: (+) *The success . . .* (usually zero article with abstract noun, although here the succeeding ET relative clauses could be read as defining, thus making use of definite article here permissible).
ll. 10—11 in vielen großartigen Unternehmungen: + *in many great/bold/noble/splendid/magnificent/grandiose undertakings/enterprises.*
l. 12 haltbar gebliebene: + *enduring;* + *preserved;* + *maintained;* + *remaining tenable.*
l. 13 Vorherrschaft: + *ascendancy;* + *superiority.*
ll. 12—13 ausgeübte: + *put into practice;* (+) *had practical expression.*

l. 13 habe: to render German subjunctive of indirect speech, insert a phrase such as: + *Ortega thought/believed/claimed;* + *in the Spaniard's view/opinion.*
l. 13 die Selbstsicherheit: + *the self-confidence;* × *the self-consciousness* (= lack of self-confidence; embarrassment; shyness). (Note definite article with abstract noun required here owing to subsequent defining relative clause; no comma.)
l. 14 verschafft: + *provided;* + *procured;* × *supplied;* × *obtained.*
l. 14 erlaubten: +*permitted;* (+) *allowed.*
l. 15 die innere Ordnung: + *the internal order;* + *the order within the island realm;* + *the interior order;* × *the inner order* ("inner" mainly for thoughts, emotions, e.g. inner man, my inner thoughts/feelings).
l. 15 des Inselreiches: + *of the island domain;* × *of the insular realm/domain* (ambiguous as could refer to insular attitude of the British towards foreign countries.)
l. 16 erachten: + *to deem [as].*

> With [his] accustomed acumen Ortega went right to the roots of the question of how that enigmatic nation had managed to gain the Englishman the reputation of being the "practical man" par excellence, although they could grant themselves the luxury of annually imprisoning a select band of talented young men — as Ortega puts it — at Oxford, where they were to occupy themselves, "beyond the relevance of time" and without any relation to practical matters, with Greek, history, and sport[s].

l. 17 mit gewohntem Scharfsinn: + *With his usual insight* ("his" obligatory); + *With [his] accustomed discernment/discrimination/sagacity/perspicacity/shrewdness* ... .
l. 18 ging der Frage auf den Grund: + *probed the question;* + *thoroughly analysed/investigated the question;* + *went [right] to the heart/core of the question;* + *got to the bottom/roots of the question;* × *went to the bottom of the question.*
l. 18 jenes rätselhafte Volk: + *that mysterious nation/people;* +*that bewildering nation;* + *that puzzling nation;* + *that inscrutable nation;* × *that obscure nation;* × *that odd nation.*
ll. 18—19 wie ... dahin gebracht habe, daß der Engländer als "praktischer Mensch" schlechthin gelten konnte: + *of how ... had managed to make the Englishman pass as ...;* + *of how ... had succeeded in making the Englishman pass as* ... .

l. 19 als "praktischer Mensch" schlechthin: + *the model "practical man".*

ll. 17—18 obgleich es sich den Luxus leistete: (a) note plural personal pronoun preferable here (reference is to nation acting as individuals, not as a collective whole); (b) + *despite the fact that/in spite of the fact that they could afford [themselves] the luxury/permit themselves the luxury/allow themselves the luxury* . . . .

ll. 20—21 eine auserlesene Schar: + *an exclusive/élite troop/host/ group/bunch;* × *a selected/chosen troop;* × *an élite horde* (too negative; does not collocate with the nature of the adjective here).

l. 21 begabter junger Männer: + *of gifted young men.*

ll. 21—22 wie Ortega sich ausdrückt: + *as O. expresses himself;* + *in O.'s words.*

l. 22 nach Oxford zu sperren: + *of locking up/of shutting up . . . at Oxford* (= university); × *in Oxford* (= city); + *of banning . . . to Oxford* (with "to ban" preposition "to" is obligatory. Thus reference is ambiguous [university or city] though fairly clear from context).

ll. 22—24 damit sie sich dort . . . beschäftigen sollten: (a) Note that if "where"-relative clause is used, comma is obligatory after "Oxford" (non-defining relative clause). (b) +, *where they were supposed to occupy themselves with . . .;* +, *where they should occupy themselves with . . .;* + *so that they might occupy themselves with . . .* (here "might" used to express "purpose" is required to translate "sollen"; "should" less likely in this purpose clause). (c) + *engage [themselves] in;* + *devote themselves to.*

ll. 22—23 "außerhalb der Zeit": a phrase which lends itself to interpretation here as its exact meaning is not clear. Such interpretations, presented in idiomatic English, as the following seem acceptable: (a) + *"irrespective of time";* (+) *"beyond time";* (b) + *"irrespective of the contemporary epoch";* + *"irrespective of contemporary trends";* (+) *"as if in another era".*

l. 23 ohne jeden Bezug zu praktischen Dingen: + *without any connection with/to;* + *without any regard to;* (+) *without any reference to practical things.*

ll. 22—24 word order: although grammatically the following word order is also permissible: (+), *where they were to devote themselves to Greek, history, and sports[s] "beyond the relevance of time" and without any relation to practical matters,* it is stylistically inferior to that offered in the "model" translation. Here the end-focus (see UGE, chapter 14: Focus, Theme and Emphasis) falls on subordinate (in ST) information ("beyond the relevance of time" and without any relation to practical matters.) and thus does not give as close a rendering of ST as the "model" translation.

> The Spaniard came close to considering this disdain for a brisk, career-orientated course of study, regarded as typical of a master ['s attitude], [as] one of the reasons for their superiority and to deriving from it that peculiar sovereignty which tends to be the mark of the British when, in later life, they play an active role. In short, Oxford reminded him of the Periclean Age with its creative freedom.

l. 25 Der Spanier: × *The Spanish* (= the whole nation); ⊗ *the Spanishman*.
l. 25 war nahe daran: + *was [very] close to ... ing;* + *was on the point of ... ing;* + *It almost happened that the Spaniard ...*.
l. 26 Verachtung: + *scorn of;* + *contempt for/of*.
l. 25 als herrenmäßig aufgefaßte: post-modification necessary in ET (see notes A 1, l. 4; ll. 18—19; A 3, ll. 9—10; ll. 16—18). + *considered typical of the ruling/upper class*.
l. 26 eines atemlosen Zweckstudiums: + *... a hectic/* + *rapid/* + *feverish/* + *hasty/* + *breathless career-orientated period of study/down-to-earth course of study;* + *... a brisk period/course of study devoted to expedient ends*. The following attempts fail as they are unidiomatic or stylistically unacceptable: × *orientated to what is of use;* × *aimed at a special occupation;* × *purpose-determined*. (Note: "study" in this sense is uncountable: thus × *a study*. To render countable add: "a period of..." or "a course of...".)
ll. 26—27 eine der Ursachen der Überlegenheit: + *... one of the causes of ...;* × *... reasons of ...*.
ll. 27—28 ... und aus ihr jene eigentümliche Souveränität abzuleiten: + *and to tracing back to the latter/to it that peculiar sovereignty...*. Take care: this infinitive clause is also dependent on the initial "Der Spanier war nahe daran, ...".
ll. 28—29 ..., die Briten auszuzeichnen pflegt,: + *which is invariably the mark of the British/of Britons;* + *which tends to be the hallmark of the British/of Britons;* + *which tends to distinguish the British*.
l. 29 später im Leben: × *in their later life/lives* (= after death).

l. 29 wenn sie ... handelnd auftreten: (a) + *when they act in life;* + *when they go out into the world;* × *when they act in public;* × *when they are acting* (the latter two suggest an acting career on the stage!) Note: it is very unlikely that this clause has the meaning: × *when they appear in the business world/* × *when they appear at the negotiating table* as this rather colloquial interpretation of "handelnd" would be incompatible with the more formal style of the text as a whole. (b) word order: Also: + *when they play an active role in later life.*
l. 29 Kurz: + *In brief;* + *To be brief;* + *Briefly;* × *Shortly* (= soon); × *To put it in a nutshell* (too informal here).
l. 30 das perikleische Zeitalter: Take care with spelling here: + *Periclean* (cf. Archimedes – Archimedean principle; Hercules – Herculean strength.)
ll. 30–31 mit seiner schöpferischen Freiheit: + *with its freedom for creativity* (+) *with its freedom of creation.* (Note: "freedom" is usually preferred (to "liberty") when qualified e.g. personal freedom; freedom of speech, action, the press. But cf. civil liberty, religious liberty.)

> Today this all looks, in some respects rather different. The most striking difference seems to lie in the fact that the British are very intensely occupied "with themselves" while the rest of the world, which their glance once encompassed, recedes to a perfectly normal distance. In so far as Ortega was already aware of the first signs of such insular alienation he sought an explanation in the changes wrought by communications, technology and revolution.

l. 32 Heute stellt sich das alles in mancher Hinsicht anders dar: + *Today everything looks quite different in many respects;* + *In many respects this all looks quite different today;* + *Today, in many respects, this all presents itself in a different light.* (Whether this sentence begins with "Today" or "This all..." is immaterial as both offer logical links.)
l. 33 Der augenfälligste Unterschied: + *The most prominent/noticeable/obvious/conspicuous/evident difference;* × *significant;* × *important.*
l. 33 aber: as no contrast is apparent do not use "however" or "but". "Aber" is used to give stress to the preceding phrase. Omit in ET.
l. 34 die Engländer: probably imprecise reference to "the British".

Also (+) *the English* (definite article obligatory with adjective used as noun to denote nationality); (+) *Englishmen* (plural noun with zero article, as reference is general).

II. 34—35 sehr intensiv "mit sich selbst" beschäftigt sind: + *are very intensely/intensively preoccupied/concerned/involved "with themselves"*.

I. 35 während die übrige Welt: + *while the remainder of the world;* + *while the world outside;* × *... the remains ....*

II. 35—36 die einst ihr Blick umfaßte: + *which was once under their close scrutiny;* (+) *which they once took in at a glance* (Suggests that the action is too superficial.)

I. 36 zurückweicht: (a) + *retreats;* + *withdraws;* + *falls back;* × *yields;* × *gives way.* (b) Use either Simple or Progressive Aspect. The latter suggests more gradual development.

I. 36 auf eine durchaus normale Distanz: + *to a completely/thoroughly/ quite normal distance/perspective.*

I. 32 Insoweit: + *Inasmuch as;* + *To the extent that.*

II. 36—37 bereits Ortega ... gewahrte: "already" cannot usually premodify a noun. Place medially within verb phrase (see "model" translation). ⊗ *became already aware;* × *already was aware* (unacceptable unless "was" is stressed for contrastive focus). See also: Schon als Kind war er sehr frech = + *As a child he was already very cheeky./* + *Even as a child he was very cheeky.* ⊗ *Already as a child he was very cheeky.*

II. 38—39 durch ... bewirkten Veränderungen: + *changes brought about by/caused by/effected by/produced by ...;* × *affected by* (= influenced by).

I. 39 Verkehr: × *communication* (= also by letter, word of mouth etc.); × *traffic* (reference too restricted); × *trade* (not in this context).

I. 39 Technik: × *engineering* (reference too restricted); × *technique* (= method).

I. 39 Verkehr, Technik und Revolution: zero article.

> He was of the opinion that the shrinking of our planet, to be observed since the end of the First World War, had gradually robbed the island realm of her unique and special position. And indeed it may be stated with good reason that Great Britain has lost the Archimedean point from which she was formerly able to maintain her system of sovereign authority in motion and in balance.

ll. 39—40 Er meinte: + *He thought/believed...;* + *In his opinion/ view...;* + *According to Ortega...;* (+) *According to him....*

ll. 40—41 die seit dem Ende des Ersten Weltkrieges zu beobachtende Schrumpfung: postmodification required (see A 1, l. 4; ll. 18—19; A 3, ll. 9—10; ll. 16—18): +*... planet, observable since the end of World War I,...;* (+) *... planet, which had been observable/which was to be observed since...* (rather too wordy); ✕ *realised* (could mean "achieved").

l. 41 Schrumpfung: (+) *the process of our planet's getting smaller* (very wordy); ✕ *contraction* (sounds too technical); ✕ *shrinkage;* ✕ *the diminishing process* (ambiguous); ✕ *shrivelling* (as dry leaves); ⊗ *the getting smaller.*

ll. 41—42 habe ... beraubt: + *had deprived her of...;* ⊗ *had robbed the unique ... position from the island realm;* (+) *had stolen from the island realm her unique ... position.*

l. 42 seiner einzigartigen Sonderstellung: (a) (+) *its* (feminine possessive determiner stylistically preferable here for reference to a nation or country in a philosophical context. See also l. 44). (b) + *of her unique and exceptional position;* (+) *of her unique, special position* (style: greater stress is afforded each of the two adjectives if linked by "and").

ll. 42—43 Und wirklich läßt sich mit guten Gründen behaupten: + *And indeed it can be argued quite reasonably that...;* + *And indeed there is every reason to state that...;* + *And indeed there are good reasons for claiming that....*

l. 44 habe ... verloren:, tense: Present Perfect only (following present tense verb introducing indirect thought.)

l. 44 den archimedischen Punkt verloren, aus dem...: (a) Defining relative clause, therefore no comma. (b) ✕ *lost its Archimedean point from which...* (Owing to presence of defining relative clause use of possessive determiner redundant here. Substitute definite article.)

l. 45 früher: + *she was once able to...;* + *she was, in former times, able to....* Word order: place time adjunct medially. Final placement would lend unnatural emphasis and steal the end-focus position from the words that require it.

ll. 45—46 in Bewegung und im Gleichgewicht zu halten: for good style in ET a parallel construction is also required as in ST: ✕ *to keep... moving and in balance;* ✕ *to keep ... moving and balanced.* + *to keep ... in motion and in equilibrium;* ⊗ *to keep ... in movement....*

Section D: A selection of examination texts

Fachliche Prüfung für das Lehramt an Realschulen, 1977/I

Die Gründerväter

Die politische Entwicklung beginnt nie vom Nullpunkt, auch nicht in einem neuen Land.
Die Männer, die die Unabhängigkeitserklärung und die Verfassung der Vereinigten Staaten niederschrieben, waren hauptsächlich Engländer, die das britische Recht und die britischen Freiheiten liebten. Wenn es in den Jahren 1775/76 in England einen weniger verbohrten König und in London eine weitblickende Regierung gegeben hätte, wäre Amerika heute vielleicht noch mit Großbritannien so verbunden wie Australien oder Kanada, und die Geschichte der Welt wäre anders verlaufen. Aber die Gründerväter der USA waren historisch gebildete Männer, Leser der Bibel, der Bücher von Gibbon und Montesquieu, geistige Erben der Aufklärung und des Jahrhunderts der Vernunft, gebildet in römischer Geschichte und durchaus informiert über die Laster, die die alte römische Republik zerstört hatten. Wenn sie das republikanische Rom der Männer wie Regulus und Cincinnatus als ihr Modell verehrten, so liebten sie doch zugleich den Geist der englischen Magna Charta und, da viele von ihnen Abkömmlinge der Pilgerväter waren, verehrten sie auch den Mayflower-Vertrag, jenes Dokument der ersten puritanischen Einwanderer, mit dem diese, noch bevor sie ihren Fuß auf amerikanischen Boden gesetzt hatten, an Bord ihres Schiffes die Grundlage schufen, auf der sie ihr "Neues Zion" regieren wollten.
Die Gründerväter, die nur bescheidene Erwartungen hegten, veröffentlichten keine flammenden Manifeste wie spätere Revolutionäre. Auch die Unabhängigkeitserklärung, die einem solchen Manifest am nächsten kam, ist ein juristisches Papier, das hauptsächlich die Übergriffe des Königs Georg III. gegen die Rechte der englischen Siedler zusammenfaßte. Die amerikanische Revolution war so erfolgreich, daß selbst Amerikaner über ihre geistige Grundlage wenig mehr wissen. Während alle Revolutionen seit damals im Namen der Freiheit zu irgendeiner Form von Terror, von "Diktatur des Proletariats" oder anderen gewaltsamen Maßnahmen ihre Zuflucht nehmen mußten, so hat sich dergleichen in den Vereinigten Staaten selbst in Kriegszeiten nie-

mals ereignet. Daß das amerikanische Regierungssystem, das eine starke Exekutive gegen eine starke Legislative ausbalanciert, neben
35 einem unabhängigen Richterstand, so hervorragend funktioniert hat, ist bei anderen Völkern im Laufe der Zeit nicht unbemerkt geblieben, und viele neue Nationen der Welt haben in größerem oder kleinerem Umfang versucht, die USA zu kopieren. Das ist oft mißlungen, vielleicht nicht so sehr weil der Apparat schlecht konstruiert war, sondern
40 weil diese Regierungsform zu Gesellschaften mit ganz anderen Traditionen nicht unbedingt paßt.

Aus: Oliver Jensen, Die ersten 200 Jahre der Geschichte der Vereinigten Staaten in "Amerika Dienst", United States Information Service, Bonn-Bad Godesberg

Fachliche Prüfung für das Lehramt an Realschulen, 1976/II

Ist aller Anfang schwer?

Aller Anfang ist schwer, wenn es sich um eine Fertigkeit handelt, also etwa ums Skilaufen, Autofahren oder Klavierspielen. Denn dann fehlt uns in der ersten Zeit eine wichtige Kraftquelle, nämlich die Übung. Ganz anders steht es, wenn wir einen Aufsatz, einen Zeitungsartikel
5 oder eine Festrede verfassen sollen. Dann haben wir ja bei den ersten Sätzen noch alle Möglichkeiten offen und es ist viel leichter, aus dem Nichts heraus zu beginnen, als eine schwierige Beweisführung folgerichtig fortzusetzen.
Freilich ist das Anfangen nur für den leicht, der einige Kunstgriffe
10 kennt. Der bekannteste Kunstgriff besteht darin, mit einem allgemeineren Begriff als dem Thema anzufangen. Wenn z. B. ein Schüler einen Aufsatz über die Rütli-Szene schreiben soll, dann beginnt er mit der Versicherung, unter allen deutschen Dichtern sei Schiller der bekannteste, von allen Dramen Schillers sei "Wilhelm Tell" das beliebteste
15 und von allen Szenen des "Tell" sei die Rütli-Szene die schönste. Das Verfahren läßt sich oft verwenden, aber es ist ein wenig abgenutzt und langweilig. Etwas besser ist der geschichtliche Einstieg. Man beginnt den Aufsatz über die Rütli-Szene mit dem Hinweis, daß die Schweiz um 1200 unter habsburgischer Herrschaft stand. Aber es wäre

beispielsweise recht mühsam, bei einem Vortrag über Kaninchenställe zuerst die Geschichte des Kaninchens und des Stallbaus zu entwickeln. Das weitaus beste und einfachste Verfahren geht nicht vom Allgemeinen und nicht von der Vergangenheit aus, sondern von irgendeinem anschaulichen Vorfall. Der Geschichtsschreiber Curtius beginnt eine Abhandlung über die olympischen Spiele mit der bekannten Anekdote, daß die Griechen auch beim Herannahen der Perser ihre Wettspiele fortsetzten und dadurch die persischen Feldherrn außerordentlich beunruhigten. Dieses Beispiel zeigt jedoch: man muß etwas wissen, um von einer bestimmten Tatsache oder einem konkreten Vorfall ausgehen zu können. Aber ohne Wissen sollte man ja überhaupt nicht schreiben.

Die allerbeste Einleitung besteht freilich oft darin, daß man auf jede Einleitung verzichtet und schonungslos mit der Tür ins Haus fällt. Alles Einfache hat eine ungeheure Gewalt. Im "Prolog im Himmel" (in Goethes Faust") will Gott der Herr auf den eigentlichen Gegenstand des ganzen Dramas zu sprechen kommen. Wie macht er das? Er sagt einfach zu Mephisto: "Kennst Du den Faust?"

Aus: Ludwig Reiners, Unsere Muttersprache (abridged)

Fachliche Prüfung für das Lehramt an Realschulen, 1975/II

Die anderen Briten

Iren, Waliser und Schotten spielen eine große Rolle im politischen und wirtschaftlichen Leben Englands. Es gibt die bekannte Geschichte von dem Schotten, der nach London fuhr, und wieder in Schottland, gefragt wurde, was er denn von Engländern halte. Ach, soll er geantwortet haben, ich habe gar keine Engländer getroffen — ich habe ja nur mit führenden Leuten gesprochen. Man hat auch gesagt, die großen englischen Kaufleute seien Schotten, die großen Musiker Waliser, die besten englischen Dichter Iren.

Ein Körnchen Wahrheit ist in alledem. Aber es gibt keine walisische Kunst (es sei denn im folkloristischen Sinne), und es gibt keine schottische Wirtschaft. Schotten, Iren und Waliser leisteten Großes, indem sie es für die soziologische Gruppe leisteten, die wir als "englisch"

bezeichnen und, genau genommen, als "britisch" bezeichnen sollten. Und trotzdem bleiben sie Schotten, Waliser und Iren. Das ist der verzwickte Sachverhalt.
Die Familie Stewart lebt seit Generationen in England. Eines Tages stellte ich Ian Stewart, einen liberalen, weltoffenen, über Kleinlichkeiten und Vorurteile hoch erhabenen Londoner Geschäftsmann, deutschen Bekannten vor als "Mr. Stewart, ein englischer Freund von mir". Ich war damals einigermaßen überrascht, als er mich sofort verbesserte: "Ein schottischer Freund, hoffe ich." Er sagte es lachend, aber man hörte doch heraus, daß es ihm ernst war.
Mit Ian Stewart machte ich meine erste Fahrt durch Schottland, die in Edinburgh anfing. Vom Schloß gingen wir die Königliche Meile entlang auf den Palast von Holyroodhouse zu, der nicht, wie das Schloß, oben auf dem Bergrücken liegt, sondern unten am Hang. Der Weg führt zunächst über die Esplanade — von jeher Schauplatz attraktiver Volksbelustigungen. Heute ist das vor allem der Große Zapfenstreich, eine Dudelsackparade bunter Uniformen im Scheinwerferlicht; früher waren es die Hinrichtungen von Rebellen. In Schottland gab es viele Rebellen.
Holyroodhouse ist nicht um seiner künstlerischen Formen willen unvergessen. Ein bißchen erinnert es, trotz den Türmen über dem Frontgebäude, an eine große Mädchenschule mit seinem viereckigen Hof, den die Staatsgemächer aus alter und jüngerer Zeit düster umschließen.

Fachliche Prüfung für das Lehramt an Realschulen, 1975/I

Stratford und sein großer Sohn

William Shakespeare würde — trotz Hilton-Hotel, Theater, Fernsehantennen, Autos und Autobussen — sein Stratford auch heute noch wiedererkennen. Dieser Ansicht sind jedenfalls die Herausgeber der Schallplatte "Shakespeare's Stratford", die Shakespeare als "den besten Führer" für das Stratford seiner Zeit anpreisen und ihn dabei gleich selbst sein Leben erzählen lassen.
Er beginnt mit seinen Erinnerungen als Fünfjähriger, die vor allem von den Tönen des Landlebens ausgefüllt sind; denn damals war Stratford

noch eine Stadt ländlichen Charakters, in der die Bauern der Umgebung ihre Eier, Äpfel und Rüben zu Markte trugen. Außer von Bienengesumm, Vogelgezwitscher und Kuhgemuh hat Shakespeare allerdings nicht viel zu erzählen. Den Rest hat eine Dame namens Rosemary Ann Sisson erfunden, um die Lücken im Leben des größten Dramatikers Englands und der Welt auszufüllen.
Dennoch trägt die Schallplatte den Stempel der Authentizität und Autorität; denn sie ist in Verbindung mit dem Shakespeare Birthplace Trust hergestellt, dessen Direktor Dr. Levi Fox darüber wacht, daß Stratford als "internationales Heiligtum" möglichst rein und würdig erhalten bleibt. Dr. Fox hat über ein Dutzend bebilderte Shakespeare- und Stratford-Führer geschrieben und setzt sich mit beachtlichem finanziellem Erfolg für seine Stiftung ein. Er ist auf seinen guten Geschäftssinn angewiesen, denn vom britischen Staat erhält der Trust keinen Penny. "Wir besitzen keinerlei finanzielle Sicherheit", klagt Dr. Fox, "aber alles ist in Ordnung, solange uns die Touristen treu bleiben." Sie tun dies nun schon seit 1847, als der Birthplace Trust von Shakespeare-Bewunderern ins Leben gerufen wurde, und nichts deutet darauf hin, daß Stratfords Bedeutung als literarische Pilgerstätte nachgelassen hätte.

Nach allem, was über ihn bekannt ist, braucht man nicht anzunehmen, daß sich William Shakespeare wegen der kommerziellen Ausbeutung seines Namens und seines literarischen Vermächtnisses im Grab umdrehen würde. Außer seinem dichterischen Genie besaß er offensichtlich auch ein gut entwickeltes geschäftliches Talent. Für einen Schauspieler und Dichter seiner Zeit gelang ihm das ungewöhnliche Kunststück, mit seinen Dramen und Theatergesellschaften nicht nur berühmt, sondern auch wohlhabend zu werden.

Aus: Dieter Schröder (Süddeutsche Zeitung 1972 — abridged)

Fachliche Prüfung für das Lehramt an Realschulen, 1974/II

Die Kunst des Picknickens

England mag dem Picknick seinen Namen gegeben haben, aber es kann wohl kaum beanspruchen, diese Form der Geselligkeit erfunden zu haben. Sie ist bestimmt wesentlich älter und muß schon lange bestanden haben, bevor auf den Britischen Inseln an derartig zivilisierte Gepflogenheiten gedacht werden konnte.

Man sollte vielleicht meinen, daß bereits Adam und Eva gepicknickt haben, da noch alle ihre Mahlzeiten im Freien stattgefunden haben. Aber zu einem Picknick gehören Gäste — und wo sollen die im Paradies hergekommen sein? Und noch eine andere Tatsache spricht gegen diese Theorie: Mahlzeiten im Garten zählen eigentlich nicht. Zu einem wirklichen Picknick muß man völlig aus der Umhegung der Zivilisation hinausgehen, hinaus in die freie Natur.

Hier muß gleich eine wichtige Einschränkung des Begriffs erwähnt werden: der wahre Picknicker darf und will sich der Natur nicht anpassen. Er muß sich gegen sie durchsetzen. Die Natur wird nur als Hintergrund, als Schauspiel, geduldet, dem man gelegentlich geneigt ist, seine Aufmerksamkeit zu schenken. Zum Zweck des geselligen Mahls im Freien behandelt der Gastgeber ein sorgfältig ausgewähltes Stück Natur, als ob es ein Teil seines Hauses wäre. Er lädt seine Gäste dorthin ein, bewirtet sie mit Speisen, die in seiner Küche zubereitet sind, und Wein aus seinem Keller (wenn er einen hat), er deckt für sie das Gras mit seinem Tischtuch und mit seinem Geschirr. Das verlangt jedenfalls der eigentliche Begriff des Picknicks.

Die Picknicks meiner Mutter waren immer ein Erfolg. "Wie machst du das bloß, daß du kaum etwas vorbereitest und daß doch immer alles klappt?" sagte ihre beste Freundin immer. Natürlich war in Wirklichkeit sehr vieles vorbereitet, und es klappte gar nicht immer alles. Aber das ist eben die Kunst des Picknickens und auch des Lebens: wenn das sorgsam Vorbereitete wie mühelose Improvisation aussieht und die aufgezwungene Improvisation wie vorbereitet funktioniert.

Selbst ein verregnetes Picknick kann die schönsten Erinnerungen hinterlassen. Und Picknicks verregnen ja doch nicht selten. Die Natur wehrt sich eben begreiflicherweise dagegen, daß man sie als Speisezimmer behandelt. Sie schüttet Wasser in den Wein, bläst Sand in die Suppe und schickt Ameisen über die Ananas. Sie will uns den Spaß verderben und weiß nicht, daß das ja gerade der Spaß ist. Sonst könnten wir ja mit unseren Gästen ebensogut zwischen unseren vier Wänden bleiben.

Rene Halkett: Hier spricht London

Wissenschaftliche Prüfung für das Lehramt an den Gymnasien, 1978/II

Das Inselvolk der Zeit Heinrichs VIII. war vorwiegend ein Bauernvolk, das sich selbst versorgte, das im Unterschied zu anderen Völkern nur wenig Handel trieb, das sich mit Seefahrt kaum befaßte. Sein Blick war weit weniger nach außen denn nach innen gerichtet. Ausdehnung
5 über die Meere hinweg kam ihm nicht in den Sinn. Anders als ihren skandinavischen Vettern und im Gegensatz zum allgemein verbreiteten Glauben, saß den Engländern die Schiffahrt keineswegs von alters her im Blut. Sie besaßen keine tief eingewurzelte Seefahrer-Tradition wie die Griechen, Italiener, Spanier und Portugiesen. Ihre Insel hatte seit
10 Anbeginn ihrer verbürgten Geschichte, mehr als tausend Jahre lang, weit abseits vom Hauptstrom des Weltgeschehens gelegen. Dieser Hauptstrom menschlichen Unternehmungsgeistes umspülte die Ufer des Mittelmeeres. Die spärlich bevölkerte Insel — zur Zeit Heinrichs VIII. lebten auf ihr noch keine zwei Millionen Menschen —, die halb
15 verloren im grauen stürmischen Nordmeer schwamm, besaß keinen Anschluß an diese Welt und hatte nur seltene und geringe Berührung mit ihr ...
Etwas von diesem vor-maritimen Lebensgefühl, ja ein gerüttelt Maß davon, wohnt dem Inselvolk noch heute inne. "Die britische Insel",
20 so hat Aneurin Bevan einmal gesagt, "ist ein Klumpen Kohle, der in einer Schüssel voller Fische schwimmt." Es gehöre, so meinte er, schon gigantischer Regierungsunverstand dazu, um es dahin zu bringen, daß es der Insel unter diesen Umständen jemals wirklich wirtschaftlich schlecht gehe. Mit dieser Vorstellung vom Klumpen Kohle
25 in einer Schüssel Fische, so merkwürdig und unschön sie sich auf den ersten Blick ausnimmt, hat es natürlich sein Richtiges. Der Reichtum in der Erde und der Reichtum im Meer müßten in der Tat von Rechts wegen den Charakter des Landes bestimmen, und in gewissem Sinn tun sie es auch: sie haben die Briten zu einem Fischer- und Seefahrer-
30 volk, zu einem Bergarbeiter- und Schwerindustrievolk gemacht. Aber das Merkwürdige ist, daß die Mehrzahl der Inselmenschen sich durchaus nicht als ein solches Volk empfindet. Es trifft zu, daß der "Klumpen Kohle" die Insel über alle Maßen industrialisiert, verstädtert und ausgesprochen "häßlich" gemacht hat; es ist richtig, daß man an keinem
35 Punkt im ganzen Land weiter als etwa hundertzwanzig Kilometer von einer Stadt entfernt ist. Aber in das tiefinnerste Lebensgefühl des

Inselbewohners ist diese Kenntnis nicht eingedrungen. Dieses Lebensgefühl sagt ihm, daß er im Grund ein "ländlicher" Mensch sei, und er lebt, als wäre er es, und erreicht mit dem hartnäckigen Festhalten an dieser Illusion, daß er es schließlich auch ist. Mit den Fischen, den Schiffen, dem Ozean verhält es sich ähnlich. Millionen der Inselbewohner kommen selten oder nie in die "Stadt", haben noch nie eine Fabrik gesehen. Millionen gleicherweise haben noch nie das Meer gesehen, werden es nie sehen und haben auch keine Lust, es zu sehen. Sie wissen, daß ihr Land eine kleine Insel ist, aber sie leben auf ihr, als sei sie ein ansehnlicher Kontinent.

Aus: Peter de Mendelssohn, Inselschicksal England

Wissenschaftliche Prüfung für das Lehramt an den Gymnasien, 1978/I

Limericks nennt man bestimmte Gedichte, die fast wie verschlüsselte Witze sind, und von der Stadt Limerick, die diesem Gedichttyp den Namen gegeben, von dieser Stadt hatte ich eine heitere Vorstellung: witzige Verse, lachende Mädchen, viel Dudelsackmusik, klingende Fröhlichkeit durch alle Straßen hin; Fröhlichkeit begegnete uns schon viel zwischen Dublin und Limerick auf den Landstraßen: Schulkinder jeden Alters trotteten heiter — manche barfuß — durch den Oktoberregen; sie kamen aus Nebenstraßen, man sah sie fern zwischen Hecken über schlammige Pfade herankommen; unzählige, die sich sammelten, wie Tropfen sich zu einem Rinnsal, Rinnsale sich zu Bächen, Bäche sich zu kleinen Flüssen sammeln — und manchmal fuhr das Auto durch sie hindurch wie durch einen Strom, der sich bereitwillig teilte. Für Minuten blieb die Landstraße leer, wenn das Auto gerade einen größeren Ort passiert hatte, und wieder sammelten sich die Tropfen: irische Schulkinder, sich schubsend, sich jagend; abenteuerlich gekleidet oft: bunt und zusammengestückelt, aber sie alle waren, wenn sie nicht heiter waren, mindestens gelassen; so traben sie oft meilenweit durch den Regen hin, durch den Regen zurück, mit Tennisschlägern in der Hand, die Bücher durch einen Riemen zusammengehalten. Einhundertachtzig Kilometer lang fuhr das Auto durch irische Schulkinder hindurch, und obwohl es regnete, viele von ihnen barfuß

waren, die meisten ärmlich gekleidet: fast alle schienen fröhlich zu sein. Ich empfand es als Blasphemie, als jemand in Deutschland mir einmal sagte: Die Straße gehört dem Motor. In Irland war ich oft ver-
25 sucht zu sagen: Die Straße gehört der Kuh; tatsächlich werden die Kühe so frei zur Weide wie die Kinder zur Schule geschickt: herdenweise nehmen sie die Straße ein, drehen sich hochmütig nach dem hupenden Auto um, und der Autofahrer hat hier Gelegenheit, Humor zu beweisen, Gelassenheit zu üben und seine Geschicklichkeit zu er-
30 proben: er fährt vorsichtig bis nahe an die Kuhherde heran, zwängt sich ängstlich in die gnädig gebildete Gasse; und sobald er die vorderste Kuh erreicht, sie überholt hat, darf er Gas geben und sich glücklich preisen, weil er der Gefahr entronnen ist; und was ist erregender, was ein besseres Stimulanz für des Menschen Dankbarkeit als eine
35 eben überstandene Gefahr? So bleibt der irische Autofahrer immer ein Geschöpf, dem Dankbarkeit nicht fremd ist; er muß ständig um sein Leben, sein Recht und sein Tempo kämpfen: gegen Schulkinder und Kühe; er würde niemals jenen snobistischen Slogan prägen können: Die Straße gehört dem Motor. Wem die Straße gehört, ist in Irland
40 noch lange nicht entschieden.

Aus: Heinrich Böll, Irisches Tagebuch

Wissenschaftliche Prüfung für das Lehramt an den Gymnasien, 1977/I

Thomas Mann hat seine Briefe kaum mit dem Nebengedanken der Edition geschrieben. Sie sind bei aller Sorgfalt intim, setzen auch das Vertrauen in den Empfänger voraus, er werde die Vertraulichkeit des Schreibers respektieren. Es gab andere, nicht wenige, die durchaus
5 auf Nachruhm beim Schreiben der Episteln bedacht waren, so bei Cicero, dem Briefpartner Caesars, der es ausdrücklich sagt, sowohl auch bei Carl Jakob Burckhardt, der mit Hofmannsthal in einer Weise brieflich verkehrte, die uns als Leser bereits miteinbezieht. Weshalb Golo Mann der Zukunft des Briefes so geringe Chancen gibt? Zum
10 Briefeschreiben gehöre Muße, gehöre die Fähigkeit, aus der Sprache neue Möglichkeiten herauszuholen, gehöre vielleicht auch die Zugehörigkeit zu einem absoluten Kreis, früher nannte man es einen "hö-

heren Stand". Zum anderen gehöre eine recht komplizierte Psychologie hinzu: ein Mittleres zwischen Einsamkeit und Geselligkeit. Es gibt zwar auch só introvertierte Briefschreiber wie Robert Musil, der an Herrn Robert Musil Briefe schrieb, die der Empfänger ebenso höflich von und an Herrn Musil beantwortete. Auch jene literarischen Tischrunden wären da zu erwähnen, bei denen man sich statt Unterhaltung gegenseitig Briefe schrieb und beantwortete.

Doch da ist noch ein anderes neben der Hast, der nivellierten Gesellschaft, dem gestörten Verhältnis zu Einsamkeit und Geselligkeit: nämlich der Verlust, zumindest der illusive Verlust der Entfernung. Wen man jeden Tag sehen könnte, oder doch zumindest morgen, dem schreibt man nicht so leicht, meint Golo Mann. Das mag wohl in seiner Banalität stimmen. Aber ist es ganz so? Kann man den trauernden Freund warten lassen, bis sich zufällig eine Gelegenheit dazu ergibt, kann man dem geliebten Menschen alles über Telefon sagen? Nicht wegen eines möglichen indiskreten Mithörers, sondern überhaupt. Zweifellos hat das Telefon viele Briefe überflüssig gemacht, vor allem geschäftliche Briefe. Aber da kommt einem doch Marie Kaschnitzs Buch "Ferngespräche" in den Sinn. Das Drama der Titelgeschichte wird in neun Telefongesprächen abgehandelt, scheinbar so, als wären sie mitstenografiert. Und doch sind es Gespräche, die so am Telefon kaum vorkommen und in ihrer Transparenz dem Brief und dem Selbstgespräch näher sind als dem durch das technische Medium notwendig und vielfach unbewußt veränderten Sprach- und Sprechverhalten. Es kann sein, daß es nach Klassizismus riecht, und doch irritiert mich die Vorstellung, daß der größte und großartigste Gedankenaustausch in unserer Sprache, der zwischen Goethe und Schiller, am Telefon abgehandelt und in Kassettenform im Handel wäre. Denn es wäre dies weder im Inhalt noch in der Form dasselbe, was uns überliefert ist.

Aus: Leonhard Reinisch, Stirbt der Brief aus? Bemerkungen nach der Herbsttagung der Deutschen Akademie für Sprache und Dichtung; in: gehört — gelesen, Dezember 1975.

Wissenschaftliche Prüfung für das Lehramt an den Gymnasien, 1976/II

Eines Tages stand ich vor dem Entschluß — da ich in meinen eigensten Bezirken, denen der Literatur und des Theaters, unverbesserlich europäisch blieb —, etwas radikal Amerikanisches zu tun, nämlich einfach und ohne Übergang einen völlig neuen Beruf zu ergreifen und
5 mein Leben damit zu fristen. Ich wurde Farmer.
Wir hatten uns zur Niederlassung den Staat Vermont ausgesucht. Uns zog dieser Staat, den wir im ersten Sommer schon als Ferienbesucher kennengelernt hatten, geradezu magisch an, und wohl nicht nur wegen seiner für uns recht heimatlichen — wenn auch allgemein wilderen —
10 Landschaft, sondern vor allem durch seine merkwürdigen, bodenständigen Bewohner, die auch für Amerikaner etwas Einzigartiges sind. Es gibt manche Amerikaner, die behaupten, der Staat Vermont sei so veraltet, daß man ihn gar nicht mehr als einen Teil des wirklichen Amerika bezeichnen könne, während die Vermonter ihrerseits erklä-
15 ren, er sei das einzige, was vom wirklichen Amerika übriggeblieben ist.
Wir waren jetzt nicht mehr Besucher, Zugvögel oder Fremdlinge, sondern Nachbarn, die mit ihren Nachbarn auf gleich und gleich zu leben hatten. Schon in der ersten Zeit begriffen wir einiges Grundsätzliche
20 und höchst Erstaunliche über das unbekannte amerikanische Menschentum. Es bestand zunächst in einer völligen Abwesenheit gewisser Züge, die uns in Europa in ähnlicher Situation bös und bitterlich aufstoßen könnte, vor allem im Fehlen der 'Schadenfreude', die übrigens die englische Sprache auch nicht als Wortbildung kennt. Niemals hatte
25 man den Eindruck, es würden sich die anderen, die eingesessenen und gelernten Farmer, ins Fäustchen lachen oder amüsieren, wenn einem etwas mißglückt, weil man es noch nicht versteht und keine Erfahrung hat. Genau das Gegenteil war der Fall. Sein Zuschauen besteht nicht darin, daß er sich grinsend die Hände reibt, sondern daß
30 er im rechten Augenblick einen Rat gibt, den man nutzen kann oder nicht. Das ist dann die eigene Sache. Und es ist noch etwas: Der Mann, der dir in einer schwierigen Situation geholfen hat, rechnet nicht auf deine ewige Dankbarkeit, sondern er findet es nur selbstverständlich, daß du im umgekehrten Fall das gleiche tun würdest. Der Nachbar, den
35 du aus dem Bett holst, weil dir dein Auto im Schneeschlamm steckengeblieben ist und er das seine vorspannen muß, um dich herauszuzie-

hen, wird weder schimpfen noch fluchen, aber er wird ohne Hemmung bei dir anklopfen, wenn ihm dasselbe passiert. Aus dieser einfachen und klaren Beziehung der Nachbarschaft in einem weiten, immer noch mit seinen Naturkräften ringenden Land wächst der Kern und der Grundstock des amerikanischen Gesellschaftslebens. Dies ist für mein Gefühl eben die einzigartige menschliche Leistung Amerikas, daß es gerade in seinem riesigen Völkergemisch und im Zug seiner höchst realistischen, harten, ja oft brutalen Geschichte solche Züge in seinem Grundcharakter entwickelt hat, von denen man wenig spricht, weil sie sich eigentlich von selbst verstehen.

Aus: Carl Zuckmayer, "Amerika ist anders"

Wissenschaftliche Prüfung für das Lehramt an den Gymnasien, 1975/I

In der Karibischen See

Wenn ein großer Schriftsteller stirbt, erinnert man sich ganz unwillkürlich des Augenblicks, in dem eines seiner Werke einem ans Herz rührte, so daß man für sein Dasein dankbar war. Das geschah mir jetzt, als ich von Eugen O'Neills Tod erfuhr. Ich hatte vor einiger Zeit etwas über ihn in der Zeitung gelesen, nach langen Jahren zum erstenmal wieder seinen Namen gedruckt gesehen. Die Nachricht war eine betrübende, O'Neill war krank, er konnte nicht mehr arbeiten, hatte es wohl die ganzen letzten Jahre hindurch nicht mehr gekonnt. Er stand jeden Morgen auf, zog sich an und setzte sich an den Schreibtisch, aber die Feder gehorchte seiner Hand nicht mehr. Er gab den Versuch auf und ließ jemanden kommen, dem er diktieren wollte, aber auch das ging nicht, da seine Zunge die Worte nicht formen konnte, die es ihn zu sagen trieb. Danach wiederholte sich jeden Morgen dasselbe, er bat allein gelassen zu werden, er blieb in seinem Stuhl sitzen und versuchte, nun wenigstens in Gedanken, die Welt zu ordnen, die in ihm nach Gestaltung verlangte. Aber auch dazu war er nicht mehr imstande, und die Besucher, die in späterer Stunde eintraten, fanden ihn zusammengesunken, mit erloschenem, völlig leerem Gesicht. Dem Bericht war eine Aufnahme beigefügt, die zu der schauerlichen

Erzählung in merkwürdigem Widerspruch stand. Es war das Bild eines gepflegten und eleganten älteren Herrn, der ein wenig Mühe hat, jung zu erscheinen — die Tragödie, die sich da alltäglich abspielte, konnte man aus den glatten, beherrschten Zügen nicht lesen, auch nicht die ursprüngliche und barbarische Kraft, mit der O'Neill die Elektrasage als eine amerikanische Familientragödie neu formte, auch nicht die Schwermut des Einakters 'In der Karibischen See', der mir bei der Nachricht von O'Neills Tod in Erinnerung kam. Aber was sind Fotografien? Als der Name O'Neills am Tage nach seinem Tode noch einmal über die Erde hinklang, hörte ich die amerikanischen Matrosen auf ihrem Schiff in der Bucht der karibischen Insel ihre gierigen und zuchtlosen Lieder grölen, ich besann mich auf die Worte des Engländers, dem es nicht gelingt, über ein früheres Erlebnis hinwegzukommen. Ich hörte ganz aus der Ferne die Gesänge der Eingeborenen, die der trostlosen Verlorenheit der jungen Amerikaner eine uralte Bindung entgegensetzen, aber eine von so schauerlicher Fremdheit, daß sie die Verzweiflung des furchtbaren Gelages nur noch erhöht. Rudolf Bach hatte das vorgelesen an einem Abend im Amerikahaus in Frankfurt, vor einigen Jahren schon. Das ist für mich O'Neill.